AN AUDIENCE OF CURIOUS PEOPLE

To Barbara,

AN AUDIENCE OF CURIOUS PEOPLE

The Story of the Proscenium Players

John Fisher

Best wishes,
John Fisher

Scratching Shed Publishing Ltd

First published by Scratching Shed Publishing Ltd in 2010
Registered in England & Wales No. 6588772.
Registered office:
47 Street Lane, Leeds, West Yorkshire. LS8 1AP

www.scratchingshedpublishing.co.uk

ISBN 978-0956252661

Unless stated otherwise, all photographs are from the personal collection of John Fisher

Cover photograph: (left to right) Stanley Sher, Cedric Gould, Alan Marshall and author John Fisher in *Pantagleize*

A catalogue record for this book is available from the British Library.

Typeset in Warnock Pro Semi Bold and Palatino

Printed and bound in the United Kingdom by
L.P.P.S.Ltd, Wellingborough, Northants, NN8 3PJ

For my mother and father, Lottie and Israel Fisher without whom I would not be here to write this book; and for Alec Baron and Cyril Livingstone without whom there would have been nothing to write about.

Acknowledgements

Compiling this book was a labour of love and I would like to thank the following for their enormous contribution: Judith Baron, for allowing me to dip into Alec's diaries, which was like going into Aladdin's Cave; Cyril Livingstone for handing over his scrapbook from the early days; Emma Gordon for proof-reading the first draft; and to my publishers Scratching Shed Publishing Ltd for their encouragement and expert advice.

Contents

Foreword

Barry Cryer OBE

Comedian, writer, performer and broadcaster Barry Cryer was fresh out of two Rag Revues at Leeds Empire when he was invited to appear in the 1955 Proscenium Players production of Elmer Rice's 1940 romantic comedy Two On An Island. *He popped up in one scene - playing a tour guide in charge of a group of visitors to Broadway - and, needless to say, stole the show.*

I have very fond memories of living in Leeds. My dad died when I was five, my brother was away in the Merchant Navy, so it was just me and my mum. We lived on Mount Pleasant Avenue, off Roundhay Avenue, off Harehills Lane.

There was a gang of us - John Andrews, Dean Tasker and David Milligan - a whole group, always on our bikes and exploring the territory. They were happy, carefree days and although my mum didn't always know where I was, she certainly knew who I was with. Today you wouldn't let a kid walk down the road to the shops but in those times we were out till dusk; it was quite safe and playing outside became part of our childhood.

I went to Leeds Grammar School followed by one year at Leeds University – Eng. Lit. Failed. You might say I blew it. I chased girls and drank a lot, and my first year's results showed it. I thought I'd let everyone down and felt awful. I had this crazy idea of being a journalist, but that was never to be. Writing was in my head but not my heart, and certainly not scriptwriting. Oh no, there was no dream of that.

I was involved in two Leeds University Rag Revues in 1955 and 1956, both at Leeds Empire. Alec Baron directed one and I directed another because Alec was indisposed; I think his mother was ill, so they shunted me in.

I will never forget two of the cast members. One was Tony Harrison, who was at University studying Classics and Literature. He was to find fame as a poet and playwright. The other was Wole Soyinka, who studied English Literature under the supervision of his mentor, Wilson Knight. Wole, who was to take his doctorate in 1973, went on to win the Nobel Prize in Literature in 1986. In the revue I remember he sang, to hilarious effect, some songs by Tom Lehrer. I wrote a lot of the material for the show. In those days everybody wrote, it wasn't anything special. And of course I got to appear in the numbers – hogging the whole proceedings, it was great. One piece stood out for me. Lonnie Donegan had recorded a song called 'Lost John' and I re-wrote the lyric. It went down very well.

It's funny how things happen; a guy came up to Leeds University to see someone in a student show, not me, but he saw me telling jokes and offered me work. So there I was with my first-year results in one hand and an offer of work in the other. I suppose that typifies the story of my life; just go with the flow. My first professional engagement was at Leeds City Varieties in 1956, some months after *Two On An Island*. Stanley and Michael Josephs, the two brothers who ran the Varieties, gave me enormous encouragement. Then I went on a regional tour in little shows and suddenly I was in showbusiness. It was all very odd; I had no intention of making this my career, it just happened.

Everybody knew about the Proscenium Players; they were 'of repute' and had built up an enormous standing for themselves in the city. Alec was terrific and so was Cyril Livingstone. Cyril should have turned professional instead of going into the Shmatter trade in North Street, but I think he stuck with it and played safe as it offered more security. I have fond memories too of Cecil Korer, with his gangly appearance and distinctive voice. I worked with Cecil professionally later on and I can recall he directed *Top Town* on BBC TV and, of course, *The Good Old Days,* with dear old Barney Colehan at Leeds City Varieties.

People today are obsessed with celebrity. I certainly don't think of myself as a star; stars get recognised. I enjoy the best of both worlds. I can walk down the street, get on a bus and, although people think they have seen me somewhere and often say 'Hello!', I can wear my cloak of anonymity. You see they think they know me, but they're not sure where from. I'm very comfortable with that.

Ronnie Corbett, my old friend, once said: 'I don't know what rung of the ladder you're on Baz, but whatever one it is just stay there.'

I remember Alec's production of *Two On An Island* because, in many ways, it pre-empted the film *Sleepless In Seattle*. The two lovers were played by Mavis Addleman and the author of this book, John Fisher. And although Mavis and John appeared in all eleven scenes, they didn't actually get together until the last, which was on top of the little lady herself, the Statue of Liberty. It was all very charming and I was really thrilled to be invited to be in the show.

I wouldn't describe what I've had as a career - just a series of incidents. I have had enormous luck all through the 50 or so years in the business, just being in the right place at the right time. I always say that if the door opens for you and you go through - you had better deliver. Just like the Proscenium Players.

BARRY CRYER, MARCH 2010

Bring up the curtain, la la la
Bring down the curtain, la la la
Bring up the curtain, la la la
Hi-ho, the glamorous life!
- The Glamorous Life
from A LITTLE NIGHT MUSIC
Stephen Sondheim, 1973

*

Preface

There was no enthusiasm towards the theatre in my family, although my mother Lottie had a wonderful soprano voice which she used to good effect.

Born in Leeds on March 12, 1904, she was only 15 when she was engaged to sing throughout the silent movies at the Victory Cinema in Camp Road. Her favourite songs were 'Because', 'Trees' and 'Second Hand Rose', which she also used to chant at charity events and soirees. However, when she married my father in 1925 he insisted that had to stop – in his opinion this songbird was getting far too much attention from the young roosters in the neighbourhood. Thereafter my mother only sang for my dad, my elder sister Veta, big brother Malcolm, for me and for anyone else in the family who was lucky enough to catch her dulcet tones.

My mum came from humble beginnings and, as the eldest daughter in a family of two boys and four girls knew what it was like to work hard. Possibly this gave her a great appreciation for the finer things in life. As a teenager in the 1950's I would accompany her in her Riley Elf to the Yorkshire stately homes that were giving up because of the iniquitous death-duties. From our jaunts to auction sales we acquired, if not the actual pieces then a love of old Chinese porcelain and Georgian furniture. Mum was also a wicked mimic and I guess this is where I inherited my hankering for acting. She was also a lot of fun and I miss her sense of humour and tinkling laugh.

My father, Israel, was born at 18 Bridge Street on December 27, 1897, in the Leylands area of Leeds. His parents were Russian immigrants and his paternal grandfather, a former cattle breeder, lived with the family and died aged 104. Dad entered his father's butcher business when he left school at the age of 12. He was a First World War veteran, serving with Leeds Pals and was badly wounded when he was 19 and had to be invalided out of the army. A hard-working man who loved his family and his business, he was keen on sport, particularly horse-racing. On a weekend he could be seen sneaking into his bedroom to phone his local bookmaker, Ruff Cramer, whispering what sounded like: 'Ruff? Butch! Six cross doubles, second favourites, Kempton Park.' He would then return to the lounge and television and spend an afternoon watching them all go down.

He told me he remembered sitting in the gods of Leeds Grand Theatre in 1920 to see Julia Neilson and Fred Terry in *Sweet Nell of Old Drury*.

Dad also smoked 40 cigarettes a day until a week before he expired at the age of 93. When he died, a customer of the same age called to say he wanted me to know that my Dad helped him financially when he was down and out but was told not to tell anyone.

I was born at 191 Chapeltown Road, in a rear-bedroom

above my father's shop, on October 4, 1937. Our family doctor, Leo Brill, had to be called out of the Paramount Theatre, at the corner of Briggate and The Headrow, to assist with my birth.

My mother always told me that he was watching Roland Young in *The Man Who Could Work Miracles,* and they had to flash an announcement over the credits to get him to reception. In 1940, the cinema and concert hall's name was changed to the Odeon, following the purchase by the Rank Organisation of all the Paramount cinemas in the UK.

In attendance at my birth was a local midwife accompanied by my Aunt Rosie, who married my father's elder brother Hyman. After my arrival, ten years after my siblings, my father took one look at me, wept, opened a bottle of whisky and got slightly drunk.

When the first sirens sounded at the start of the Second World War my mother panicked and, picking me up from my cot, ran the whole length of Cowper Street where there was a public air-raid shelter. However, a woman called out to return home as the shelter was full and an army of Nazis was marching up The Headrow. Fortunately neither piece of information proved true, and my mother and I returned to home and safety.

When I was five we moved to 17 Mexborough Avenue, a much bigger residence and room enough for a family of five plus my maternal grandfather, Lesser Samuel Levi - a German Jew who came to this country at the end of the 19th century. We also had a baby grand piano, a Decca radio-gramophone, a home-movie projector and screen and a gorgeous wire fox terrier called Judy. My father loved gizmos and gadgets and we collected lots of records. We had the 'Warsaw Concerto', Tchaikovsky's 'Piano Concerto No 1', Frank Sinatra singing 'I Couldn't Sleep a Wink Last Night', 'My Yiddisher Mamma' (Sophie Tucker singing in English and Yiddish) Artie Shaw playing 'Begin the Beguine' and the polka and fugue from *Schwanda the Bagpiper*.

Living opposite us, at number 25, was a charming lady called Nina Cohen, a gifted pianist who used to give evening lessons in our lounge to my brother Malcolm. I fondly remember him playing Schubert and Brahms as I tried to sleep. The music filtered up to my room; his playing was very beautiful, but Malcolm never continued with his study of music which was a shame. I longed to play the piano, but by the time I was seven the baby grand had been sold along with the home-movie unit and the gramophone. Thankfully we kept Judy who was to give birth shortly afterwards to four pups. We kept one, a frisky little feller called Terry and I just adored him. By now the War was coming to an end but times were still tough.

I was an imaginative child who always loved performing. I remember once tap-dancing on the kitchen table when I was eight after I had seen Fred Astaire in *Top Hat*. My father wasn't too pleased. I remember I had a penchant for improvised dancing which I used to do on our annual summer holidays at Freeman and Bowman's boarding house in Blackpool. My mother used to encourage me to perform for the guests who gathered in the lounge after the evening meal. Obviously they had no other form of after-dinner entertainment but when I think of it now, I go into a cold sweat with embarrassment.

The first play I ever saw was *The Browning Version* at Leeds Grand Theatre, starring Eric Portman and Mary Ellis. I was taken by my mother's sister Eva and we sat on the first row of the stalls which Aunt Eva thought to be very grand. I was transfixed and thought the acting was breathtaking.

I was also quite a film-buff. I once saw *The Thief of Baghdad* on three consecutive nights at the Forum cinema on Chapeltown Road. On the final outing I accidentally swallowed my chewing gum during the thrill of it all and ran out of the cinema in sheer panic just as Sabu was climbing a huge web and fighting off a giant guardian spider.

When we moved north to Broomhill Drive in Moortown, the Kingsway cinema became my regular haunt and I practically lived there. I remember attending weekly matinees and because I was under-age I was forbidden to view films categorised 'A' (adults only) unless accompanied by an adult, so I used to ask a very charismatic lady: 'Please would you take me in?' I would give her my one shilling and nine pence and once we were past the glare of the box-office cashier I could sit wherever I wanted. This lady, whose name I never knew, became my regular contact and complied for every film I wanted to see except one, *A Streetcar Named Desire*. 'I am sorry, young man,' she scolded, 'this film is definitely not for you!' and in she sailed without me. I felt terribly abandoned. Those were such innocent times but I rather think our weekly liaison would be frowned upon in today's politically correct scenario.

At the weekends my mother gave me the choice of the Scala, the Ritz, the Tower, the Odeon or the Majestic cinemas. We both had a fondness for Abbott and Costello and Hollywood musicals starring Carmen Miranda, Betty Grable and Don Ameche, but for something more dramatic we would plump for Joan Crawford, Bette Davis, Humphrey Bogart or Edward G. Robinson.

Years later, I had a regular seat at Leeds Theatre Royal to see Harry Hanson's famous Court Players. As a young lad I was intrigued to see the same actors playing different characters each week and, in some strange way, I learned a lot about acting from this continual observation. Needless to say, I was never away from Leeds Grand Theatre where a fine display of West End acting and drama was always on offer.

Above: John Fisher as Dr Knock, with Renee Hipshon, in *Dr Knock*, February 1958

In those days theatrical icons such as Gielgud, Richardson, Redgrave, Thorndike and the rest came on tour; it went with the territory. Those were golden days for Leeds.

As a boisterous 12-year-old I was sent by my mother to an elocution teacher called Jean Collins. The reason was not because mum thought my speech needed correcting but because my 13th birthday was looming and she had heard Jean wrote marvellous speeches for Bar Mitzvah boys.

So off I went to see Jean at her home in Chapel Allerton. She immediately asked me to read some prose and after remarking 'that's rather good' thrust a John Masefield poem under my nose and once I had waded through it said 'that's even better' and speedily entered me into a drama competition. So, the monthly lessons to learn my Bar Mitzvah speech were quickly set aside for a weekly workshop of Walter de la Mare, Rupert Brooke and rehearsals for the London Academy of Music and Dramatic Art (LAMDA) examinations.

Sometime later, Jean suggested I audition for BBC's *Children's Hour*, which was broadcast from Manchester. I was amazed to win especially as I was one of ten children chosen out of some 650. Another Jean Collins pupil to win was Carol Ableson, who lived near to me, and we travelled together to the BBC studios in Piccadilly.

We had both met when I was taking my first LAMDA examination in a musty room in the Belgrave Central Church Hall, just off New Briggate. It was a cold, foggy day in November 1951 and Carol, who was taking her fourth examination, was first to go through the double doors, ultimately returning with a distinction in elocution. Carol had a mother called Rose (why are all backstage mothers called Rose?) a small woman with a big heart and a deep, husky voice, cultivated over many years by heavy smoking. Rose was delighted with her daughter's result. However, when I emerged later with an Honours in Junior Acting she gasped and applauded as if I'd just been presented with a BAFTA.

Anyway, when Carol and I eventually appeared on radio Rose was convinced that we were both heading for Hollywood. Given the chance I feel sure she would have been our agent if the job had been offered to her.

Carol and I featured in a play called *Adventure with the Arkwrights* written by Margaret Potter and we acted alongside an unknown Eileen Derbyshire, who was later to be cast as Miss Nugent in a new TV soap opera called *Coronation Street*. Also in the broadcast was a delightful, bubbly presenter called Judith Chalmers and Herbert Smith, a grand veteran character actor with a rich, fruity voice. I was cast as Arkwright junior but longed to play the sort of senior characters that Herbert was playing.

My voice was just starting to break and the BBC must have been pretty desperate because I sounded like a cross between Katharine Hepburn and Donald Duck. Nevertheless, I was invited to make a return visit a few weeks later to play in the Arkwright saga, mark two.

Soon after, flushed with success, I telephoned a man well known on the Leeds theatre scene, Alec Baron, to ask his permission to attend an audition for a forthcoming Proscenium Players production. I had been told about the casting of Yvonne Mitchell's *The Same Sky* by Stuart Scott, a school friend who lived near Cyril Livingstone, owner of a ladies fashion shop. Cyril, who was a member of the Proscenium Players - better known locally as the Pross - had invited him to read for the part of Manny Brodsky in Mitchell's play about inter-marriage.

Given Alec's well-established theatrical reputation, I put on a very deep and resonant voice over the phone. My brother overheard me and went into fits of laughter, teasing me for weeks on end about my 'actor's voice'.

I can recall the actual Pross casting for *The Same Sky* quite vividly; it was in Room 3 of the Leeds Civic Arts Guild rehearsal rooms in Cookridge Street and held on a Sunday afternoon at 2.30pm. One had to climb a steep flight of stairs, continue through the canteen and then ascend another flight of stairs to get there. It was rather a large room with a stage in one corner and an ante-room in another. I was terribly naive and somewhat overawed by it all. I had never been in the presence of 'real' actors before, but there was this tremendous buzz of theatre talk, gossip and laughter that appealed to me as well as an assortment of interesting people.

I thought I read the part of Manny rather well and knew I made an impression because I sensed people turning round to look at me approvingly. However, I didn't get the part. Stuart eventually was cast as the 13-year-old East End kid, but I was disappointed. Nevertheless, I received a charming hand-written letter two days later from the group's vice-chairman Maxwell Saunders, who wrote: 'Although we felt you were too old for the part of Manny, the committee was highly impressed with your reading and we feel confident that in the fullness of time your talents will be used to great advantage in future productions'.

That letter opened the floodgates and true to Max's word I was given a small part in the Pross' next production of *The Relapse* or *Virtue in Danger* and cast as a grotesque country bumpkin whose first lines I can still recall today:

> Nurse, go thy ways and ask Sir Tunbelly if he chooses
> to be waited upon. And, dost hear, call to Nurse that
> she may lock up Miss Hoyden afore the gates open.

This was delivered with more than a touch of Robert Newton as Long John Silver and appeared to amuse everyone.

That role led to me being cast as the prematurely aged Peter Shirley in Shaw's *Major Barbara*, the part that set me off on a 25-year journey in amateur dramatics that I never really wanted to end. Through the amateur stage movement I have had the good fortune to work with amazing people, to forge life-long friendships and to act with one of the best drama groups in the country.

I hope this book illustrates what a joy amateur drama can be and inspires some youngster to join a local drama group – if he or she is just a little bit creative and interested in theatre it is the best hobby to cultivate.

These were certainly the happiest days of my life.

JOHN L FISHER

Above: The inaugural Proscenium Players production, *The Little Foxes* (1948)

To Begin At The Beginning
Under Milk Wood

The year 1948 was a momentous one. The State of Israel was founded, Mahatma Gandhi was assassinated and the British National Health Service was launched. The year was also significant for one Yorkshire man returning to the routine of home life after serving his country during World War Two.

In those austere days, returning to normality, however small, was not always an easy task. If they were fortunate each member of the forces had private aspirations of what he or she was going to do for the rest of their lives. Some felt it had interrupted their education or spoilt their chances for a decent career. It certainly unsettled a young man from Leeds called Alec Baron, who had spent most of his adult life selling clothes that his father, a tailor, had made. But this talented market salesman had other ideas. So passionate was he about the world of cinema and theatre, that Alec had ambitions about making either one of these his chosen career.

Alec was born on November 29, 1913 and as a schoolboy was helped by a group of close friends to form the Dramatic

Arts Club, which was to meet every Friday for several years in alternate houses to discuss the arts. The same group of teenagers also started Leeds Film Group, showing art house films in German, Russian and French.

Alec hankered for a life in film or theatre and had already started his own theatre company called Astra. At that time, drama in the regional areas of Britain was sadly lacking and for a taste of the real stuff one had to move to the great Metropolis.

Prior to his going into the forces he became fascinated by the work of Unity Theatre, which operated from Kings Cross in London, and was keen to launch a similar venture in Leeds. Along with some literary friends from the Left Book Club Forum and a few theatrical friends from Leeds, he formed a committee in the late 1930s with the idea of creating a small theatre; not only for the home of the Leeds branch of Unity but one that would also incorporate the LBCF. The most suitable accommodation, at an affordable rental, was a complete top floor of empty rooms along Park Lane, near the old dilapidated premises from where the LBCF operated. Alec purchased 100 upholstered tip-up seats at a bargain price of half a crown each, from the Little Theatre in Leeds, which had recently closed down. Before long he had managed to make a comfortable little 100-seat theatre with an adequate lighting rig. Entry to the shows was one shilling, as was the membership fee. Most of the plays were political and left wing and included works by Clifford Odets, Bernard Shaw and Sean O'Casey.

Together with Kate Plenty, Alec had written a play called *Comrade Enemy* which had received a four-month run at Unity in 1942 and was much admired by Dame Sybil Thorndike and Herbert Marshall.

However, the outbreak of the Second World War quickly put paid to Alec's theatrical dreams as well as his work with

Leeds Unity; and after he was called up for army service Kate Plenty took over. Following his initial training at Catterick Camp Alec served his time in the army.

When he was demobbed and came home his wish was to travel to London and find work in the theatre, but his family was not too keen. They warned that all he had was his discharge money and to go to London would be ill-conceived and foolish. They advised him to find work in Leeds, where tailoring was booming, and save his hard-earned money for future enterprises.

Alec realised the good sense in his family's directive and returned to working in the markets. There was such a shortage of good clothes that the only problem appeared to be getting further supplies. Moreover, he felt a sense of personal loss because, after his demobilisation, his beloved Leeds Unity Theatre had closed down in 1945.

Nonetheless, his burning love of theatre could not be fanned down and he decided to make local theatre his hobby. Some months later, he began anew under the name of Leeds Citizens Theatre, which was advertised as the 'Leeds Branch of Unity Theatre Society Ltd'. Alec produced a handful of plays including *God Bless the Guv'nor*, a Victorian melodrama in three acts with an anti-drink and trade union theme. The play was staged at the newly-equipped theatre Priestley Hall in City Square and was mischievously advertised on the hoardings as being under the patronage of 'The Duke of Hunslet'. In the cast were George Cooper, Rosa Taylor and Mona and Anita Surr, two sisters who were destined to become Alec's life-long friends.

The aims and objectives of Leeds Citizens Theatre were: 'To foster and further the art of drama in accordance with the principle that true art, by effectively presenting and truthfully interpreting life as experienced by the majority of people, can move the people to work for the betterment of society'.

An Audience of Curious People

The Society quickly followed *God Bless the Guv'nor* with *Starched Aprons,* a medical play by the Scottish writer Ena Lamont Stewart. Both were staged under Alec's direction. For this production, the Society moved into the Albert Hall on Cookridge Street for two performances on July 19 and 20. Staying with the same company of thespians, Alec also included two local actors, Cyril Livingstone and Cecil Korer. The stage manager was Jean Webber and the sets were designed and executed by Tom Coward and Peter Brackup.

About this time, Jewish charity groups were being established in order to raise funds for the newly-formed State of Israel and a local Jewish organisation approached Alec to direct a play for them at the Leeds Jewish Institute in Savile Mount. Alec chose Clifford Odets' *Awake and Sing,* a play about the problems of a New York Jewish family during the Depression. Esta Stein, a well-known professional actress from the Yiddish Theatre, had settled in Leeds and agreed to play the part of the mother, Bessie Berger. As this was an independent group, and far removed from The Citizens Theatre, the players announced themselves as the 'Leeds Jewish Institute Theatre Group'.

So successful was the event that the charity committee asked for another production and Alec hit on the idea of staging Lillian Hellman's study of greed and corruption, *The Little Foxes.*

The company had been gathered together by Alec and a close friend Iris Barrett and comprised of a small band of local actors including Cyril Livingstone, Cecil Korer, Doreen Barnett, Vivienne Jacobs, Zelda Black, Gerald Coleman, Leslie Rosen, Minnie Marks, Rosalyn Whyman and a newcomer called Max Gordon. Once again, Leeds Jewish theatregoers packed the hall and were thrilled with the results; the production was an unqualified success. It was presented once more at the Leeds Jewish Institute on

Monday and Tuesday April 26, 27, 1948, and sponsored by a young Zionist crowd called 'The Leeds Young Women's Zionist Group', chaired by Vera Pearce. A message of appreciation was sent by the chairman of Leeds Women's Zionist Council, Gertrude Rosenthal, who wrote: 'This young women's group is doing yeoman work for Palestine, and must feel an immense satisfaction that they are helping their brothers and sisters, whose role is so hard, and who are facing their vicissitudes so bravely'.

The day after the show closed Alec received a phone call from Max Gordon. Max's wife Joan had been script secretary for the show and thought the talent and enthusiasm of the enterprise needed developing. She suggested the idea of setting up a Jewish drama group. Max telephoned around the company and put the idea to them. The consensus was that they should go ahead with the suggestion and they proposed that Alec come in as resident director. Max contacted Alec, who asked to sleep on the idea before agreeing to a preliminary meeting held at 281 Harrogate Road, the home of Max and Joan.

At this gathering Alec announced that he was certainly interested in the concept of forming a drama group, but had a few misgivings and stipulations to impose. Firstly, he was not interested in a theatre group that was open to all and sundry, for he had no desire to work with people who were neither dedicated nor talented or who joined purely for a social outlet. Every member, he said, would have to be carefully selected before being invited to join. They must have a proven talent for acting, designing, set building, costume making or at least possess one of the many skills required in the theatre. Above all, he maintained they must have a passion for theatre and be prepared to work hard and give total commitment.

Nine people turned up for that auspicious meeting,

mainly actors Alec had worked with previously, whose integrity and ability he was familiar with. These included Max and Joan Gordon, Iris Barrett and Doreen Jackson, who had been assistant stage manager on *The Little Foxes*. Cyril Livingstone, an enthusiastic, talented actor with a keen desire to direct and Cecil Korer, later to become a TV producer and Commissioning Editor for C4. Myer Steinberg and Lionel Poyser, both experienced middle-aged actors, completed the working group. A committee was elected, with Iris as secretary. After a long, hilarious meeting where almost every permutation of theatrical label was tried and tested, it was finally decided to go with the name: THE PROSCENIUM PLAYERS.

Iris, who was to marry Archie Haller some years later and whisked off to a new life in Kenya recalls: 'It took us ages to think up a name for the group – it was tremendous fun. I enjoyed getting everyone together and persuading them to participate in the play. I don't think you get that sort of camaraderie anywhere else but from a group of creative people. They really were a wonderful troupe with some first -class people. But we were given a set of strict rules that had to be adhered to. The aims of the society were twofold. Firstly, to produce plays of artistic merit not normally presented by the commercial theatre; and secondly to perform plays with a Jewish interest.'

The group chose the Leeds Albert Hall as their venue and resolutely decided upon the onerous task of presenting four productions a year.

At last, Leeds' first Jewish drama group was born.

We Don't Live Alone.
We Are Members Of One Body.
An Inspector Calls

The Albert Hall was situated inside a building in Cookridge Street, which was built in 1868 as the Mechanics Institute (the Institute of Arts and Science). The venue was an imposing building and designed by Cuthbert Brodrick, the Leeds architect who had designed the Town Hall and the Corn Exchange. The main feature of this building was a circular lecture hall, called the Albert Hall, with a gallery supported by cast iron columns. In addition to this excellent facility there was a library, classrooms and reading rooms, and on the first floors an art gallery. Further rooms were used by the School of Design and Art.

In 1903, the School of Art moved out and the educational functions of the Institute were transferred to other buildings, although the Institute Library remained, as did the City of Leeds College of Music. In the early 1920s the hall began to be used as a theatre and, in 1925, the Civic Playhouse, affiliated to the British Drama League, opened in the Albert Hall with a performance of Sutton Vane's comedy, *Overture.*

An Audience of Curious People

In 1949, a cinematically designed stage, completely out of keeping with Brodrick's original concept, was constructed in the Albert Hall. It obscured the ornamental ceiling in the lecture hall and part of the scrolled balustrade was removed. After its complete make-over, the Albert Hall was officially opened in 1950 as Leeds Civic Theatre, by the Lord Mayor of Leeds, Alderman F.H.O'Donnell, JP.

Initially, membership of the Proscenium Players was limited to 25 and by audition only. However, as productions became more ambitious, it was decided to open up the membership to the wider community and avoid missing valuable artistic talent.

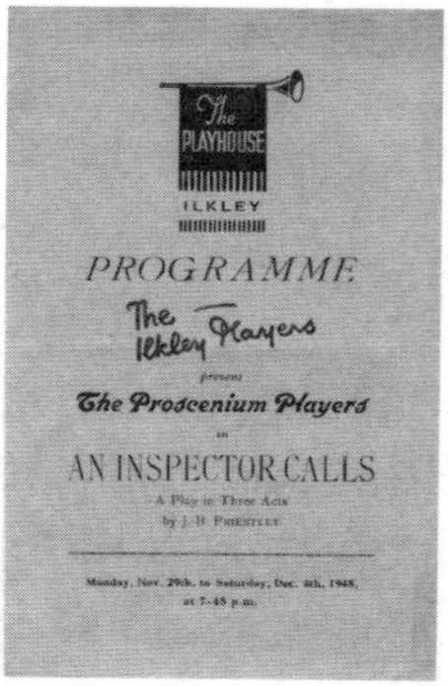

Committee meetings were always held at the home of Max and Joan and the get-togethers often continued until the early hours of the morning. This set the standard for a format that continued for many years to follow, where the encounters became a gathering for theatre talk, gossip, much-heated debates and, of course, a lot of hard work. The ambience was laced with wit and humour and lots of laughter; a priceless heritage indeed.

Castings of plays were hilarious and at times blatantly personal. Men were constantly in demand and their acting limitations totally dismissed. On one occasion, Alec decided he wanted to cast an actor whom he last saw ten years previously getting on a tramcar outside Marks and Spencer, in Briggate. Various searches were instituted without success, until someone hit on the idea of discovering which area the tramcar served. A few people who lived in those districts were contacted and enquiries made about the whereabouts of the man. Needless to say, he was eventually tracked down, but the years had not been kind to him. His

Above: The Pross followed *An Inspector Calls* with *Our Town*

interest in amateur theatre had failed, and so, unfortunately, had his memory.

The Players' debut production was JB Priestley's *An Inspector Calls*. Alec had recently seen a production of the play in London's West End and in his usual formidable style decided that the show's director had 'not quite got it right'. Alec was determined to do it better and set the room in which the action takes place on a bright yellow cloud-shaped carpet. Outside this space was a tree, and beneath its branches stood the imposing figure of the Inspector. The play was cast from within the company's own limited membership plus one guest, an actress called Pamela Cowan who later turned professional and achieved some success. Cyril Livingstone designed the costumes and Marie Richardson, a friend of actress Renee Horwich, was called in to assist with the sewing.

Waterman's, the jewellers in Briggate, agreed to look after the ticket sales and opened up a corner of their shop as the box office. Harry Waterman's daughter, Fanny, a pianist, was later to become co-founder of the Leeds International Pianoforte Competition.

The play was staged at the Albert Hall for two performances, on November 2 and 3, 1948. Again Alec and his committee turned to a charity group for sponsorship, this time the Leeds Workers' Circle, Poale Zion. They were to be the first charity group to be associated officially with the Proscenium Players and were delighted to receive a cheque for £200 from the group.

The *Yorkshire Evening Post* reviewer wrote of the play:

> When the Proscenium Players last night made their debut with *An Inspector Calls,* the Albert Hall was packed to capacity with an audience of curious people. They didn't know what to expect; they were prepared for the worst and hoped for the best. Their hopes were soon justified for after the first act the audience knew that they were witnessing a production of promise. The audience was spellbound from beginning to end, and had the proverbial pin dropped I feel sure that it would have been heard.

The two performances at the theatre proved to be a palpable hit and the company was invited to take the show on tour for a further week at nearby Ilkley Playhouse, on Monday-Saturday, November 29-December 4, 1948.

Iris Haller recalls hunting round Leeds for some fine furniture for the set. 'I went to see Manny Cussins because we wanted a dining room suite. I saw a beautiful Chippendale style table and chair that looked very grand but he was reluctant to let it go. However, I was determined to have that furniture and eventually persuaded him to loan it to us.'

Although often referred to as the Albert Hall the building ultimately became known as Leeds Civic Theatre. It not only developed into a place where plays were performed, but was also used as a training ground for budding actors eager to learn their craft. It was also a haunt for talent scouts from the BBC and the professional stage.

One of these hopefuls was a young man, aged 17, whose first job was wrapping cartons in a warehouse. He made his amateur stage debut at the theatre in a production of *A Month in the Country*, directed by David Giles. At the age of 14 he joined the *Yorkshire Evening Post*, working first as a messenger and copy boy and then as a trainee journalist and photographer. His name was Peter O'Toole.

One of the founder members was the aforementioned Cecil Korer who, many years later, became a TV producer. He would go on to direct the BBC's *Top Town* - predecessor to the legendary *It's a Knockout* - and become known as TV's 'Quiz King'. Cecil produced many programmes that today are regarded as classics, like *Jeux San-Frontiers, The Good Old Days, Ask the Family* and *Countdown*. In fact, Cecil is the CECIL after which CECIL, the electronic calculator, in *Countdown* is named. He recalled: 'I was approached to join the Pross in 1948; an invitation that would eventually shape the rest of my life and career. I was both flattered and delighted to join the group, not only did I love acting but it reunited me with some old friends from my days at Leeds Unity Theatre.'

Tall and thin, Cecil had an almost comical appearance and was always assured of a warm response whenever he appeared on stage and where he inevitably played for laughs. 'Very slowly we began to be recognised as one of the leading groups in Yorkshire, mainly because of the brilliant direction of Alec Baron and later on by Cyril Livingstone,' he went on. 'We became one big happy family and would often meet up for coffee in Schofield's department store to plan where and how we were going to convene socially. We infuriated a lot of people with our closeness and Bohemian behaviour - in fact we became known as 'The Obscenium

Players' - uninhibited in thought, deeds and our approach to life.'

By this time Alec had developed a special interest in the Stanislavsky method of acting and, apart from directing the company's first few plays, held quite a few drama classes and workshops. This method of directing spilled over into the company's main body of work. As soon as a play went into rehearsal the company held a complete analysis. This usually extended to actors and technical staff, so that everyone in the company knew what the production's objectives were. The play was always to be 'the thing' and was deemed to be more important than any one individual actor. Alec felt that a lengthy investigation was vital before blocking was done, so that there was a total understanding of what the play, the playwright's intentions and the director's aims were all about.

This meant that the company had to be completely *au fait* with the drama before it attended the analysis. Once there, they would sit in a semi-circle and each would begin to relate the story of the play, elaborating on the playwright's intention, why the play had been written, where the climax came, what scenes most impressed and in what style the play should be presented.

In the early days it was customary to rehearse in the Leeds Civic Arts Guild's rehearsal rooms in Cookridge Street but, as rehearsals had to finish at 10pm, the company often went back to each other's homes to continue working. Alec was a hard taskmaster especially about learning lines.

'Unless you know the part forwards, backwards and inside-out, don't bother coming to rehearsals, because until the lines become part of you, an actor cannot start to create a character', he told his company.

They Don't Understand, Do They?
Our Town

An Inspector Calls was followed almost immediately with a production of Thornton Wilder's *Our Town*, a play set in Grover's Corner, a small provincial town in America. Alec refused to tax his actors with phoney American accents and daringly adapted the play, without permission, into a local setting suggesting the actors adopt a mild Yorkshire dialect instead. Grover's Corner became Grover's Bridge, based on Sowerby Bridge a small town near Leeds. He presented the play in a stylised manner, in a wide-open space without props and scenery and with imaginative use of lighting.

Staging the production at the Albert Hall for two nights, 21 and 22 December 1948, the company's sponsorship came from another young charity group of Zionist women called The Blanche Dugdale Group.

On the first night, ten minutes before the final curtain, there was a backstage drama. The ancient pot dimmers in the theatre's lighting rig could not cope with the extra load that had been designed and the acid almost bubbled away. The electrician in charge of lighting the play was afraid the whole switchboard, in the wings, would go up in flames and suggested he turn off the lights immediately. Alec was at his wits end and cried out: 'Don't you understand, terminating the play now would ruin the performance.' Almost forcibly restraining him, Alec insisted the play continue to its climax, which it did without further incident.

In a half-page review in the *Yorkshire Post* the following morning, the bold headline declared: 'Another Triumph for the Proscenium Players.' The drama critic heaped praise on a young actor called George Cooper, who was cast in the plum part of the Stage Manager / Narrator, stating: 'We don't know who you are, Mr. Cooper, or what you are, but you certainly know how to act!'

George, who was the first non-Jewish member to be invited to join the company, was an architect working in the Leeds City Architects Department and passionately interested in acting. He had worked with Alec back in the days of Citizens Theatre and hearing of the Pross' already growing reputation had applied for membership, auditioned and finally won a place, not only in the society but in the Players' hearts as well. He was soon to turn to the professional stage and apart from many appearances in the West End, particularly as the father in the London production of Keith Waterhouse's *Billy Liar*, he also appeared regularly as the caretaker in BBC TV's *Grange Hill*. Rosalyn Whyman, as Emily, was also praised and the reviewer commented that 'her performance was of such a high standard that it cannot go by unmentioned'.

Rosalyn says: '*Our Town* was such a beautiful play. It was charming and, oh, I don't know, just lovely. I adored George Cooper, a really sound actor, but he was murder to act with. He did the most diabolical things. In the wedding scene the guests were all facing upstage. Peter Taylor and I were the young couple getting married and we stood in front of the guests facing the vicar, played by George. He used to make the most outrageous remarks under his breath which reduced us all to fits of giggles. He was very naughty. However, this was the play that made me feel I had discovered an extended family, so strongly did we all bond together. They were halcyon days.'

Around this time Judith Edelston, who was to marry Alec Baron many years later, had enrolled in the North of England College for a six-month course at shorthand and typing prior to university. On the same course she met Pamela Cowan who introduced her to Jacqueline Steinberg and Harry Hurst. All three were involved in a new Jewish drama group and were eager to share their excitement about the Proscenium Players.

Judith said she had already seen the group's inaugural production *The Little Foxes* and, spurred on by this, went to see them again in *An Inspector Calls*. During a break for lunch they had gathered in the Kardomah, a favourite coffee drinking haunt, which was situated in the city centre. The talk turned to the Pross' latest production.

Judith recalls: 'Pamela told me they were short of front-of-house staff and invited me to sell programmes for Thornton Wilder's *Our Town*. I enjoyed the feeling of being involved with theatre, however marginal, so I agreed. I then started to attend rehearsals where I met other members of the group - I didn't know then but this was to affect my whole life.'

Judith first met Alec Baron at rehearsals but the couple didn't connect instantly. 'We didn't start going out together until much later. In fact, Alec was the only member of the Pross committee to say "no" when my name was put forward to become a member. Somewhere in the minutes is written: "Everyone agreed Judith Edelston should become a member -- except Alec Baron".'

An Audience of Curious People

In between the Wilder play and the next production, the Pross participated in the Festival of Jewish Drama at the Devonshire Theatre in Manchester, eventually reaching the finals, but failing to come away with top prize.

The play was called *A Greater Glory* by Samuel J.Citron, and the competition was run by the British Drama League in Ilkley. It gave a glimpse of life in a pioneer Palestine settlement. Iris Barrett, playing opposite Cecil Korer, turned in an exceptional performance as the wife of a young Polish doctor. The *Amateur Stage* magazine critic commented that the Pross had provided a powerful naturalistic setting and Iris had given 'a beautiful performance' as the young wife and Cecil played with 'a quiet power'. It went on:

> The Leeds group the Proscenium Players is one of the finest amateur teams seen in Manchester in years. But for one technical flaw it might easily have run away with the Festival.

Iris recalls one panic-stricken moment. 'As the nurse, I had to wear a starched white nurse's uniform. We had done the play in Ilkley and a few days later travelled across the Pennines to Manchester. Soon after I arrived I realised to my horror that I had left my costume in the dressing room in Ilkley. I dare not tell Alec, he would have gone mad at my incompetence. I just didn't know what to do, so without telling anyone I got into a taxi and requested the driver take me to the Manchester Jewish Hospital and asked to see the Matron, who received me in her office.

'With tears in my eyes I told her of my predicament. She was so sympathetic and charming and immediately loaned me a beautifully laundered white coat and sent me on my way with good luck messages. She really saved the day and Alec was none the wiser.

'I was very close to Alec, a real man of the theatre. He loved drama and music and I adored going to the opera with him, just to see what he got out of it. The way he talked about the productions was enthralling; he saw such detail that had completely escaped me and I don't think I would have been aware of it had I gone with anyone else. I think if he had been born a generation later I am sure he would have been able to get into the theatre professionally and done some outstanding work there. We all learned so much from him.

'*Glory* was the only play I ever did for the Pross because soon after this I left for America to visit paternal relatives. I went out on the Queen Elizabeth and what a ship that was. You can imagine what that was like; remember this was during a period of great austerity in Britain. The food on the table was groaning and the place was like a floating Grand Hotel. I was just like one of the Bisto kids going round from room to room in absolute awe.

'I was only back two days when I was invited to a wedding and met Arthur Haller. In a funny sort of way that trip to America gave me the confidence to travel to other parts of the world, and when after a short courtship Arthur proposed and I had the chance to go and live in Kenya I seized the moment. Arthur and America made me realise there were further horizons to explore and life became very exciting indeed.

'When I got on the ship to go to Mombasa there was a gorgeous bouquet of flowers waiting for me from my friends in the Pross and a lovely little poem that Cyril had written with something about hoping when you return you'll bring back your own productions. It was very sweet and touching and I kept that note for years.'

Sometime later the group presented the play at The Jubilee Hall for a Jewish Festival held on March 17, 1949.

Above: A scene from *You Can't Take It With You* (M. Hart, George S. Kaufman - 1949)

Meanwhile, back at the Albert Hall, the company followed their new-found success with a production of Kaufman and Hart's *You Can't Take It with You*, this time with American accents. The play ran for three performances on April 25-27, 1949, and was the final production of the group's enormously successful first season.

It boasted a cast of nearly 20 actors which, by this time, was no problem because local actors were queuing up to play an active part in this new, energetic and vibrant amateur company. George Cooper was once again cast in a leading role and, for this production, Alec taught him to play the xylophone so that George could accompany actress Jacqueline Steinberg as she did her ballet dancing around the stage. Cecil Korer gave a memorable performance as Boris Kolenkhov with an amazing Russian accent and Rosalyn Whyman again delighted as the ingénue, Alice.

'Here I am a vision in blue!' she said. This phrase haunted Rosalyn for many years to come and whenever she went to a party this was the first greeting thrown at her as she entered a room. *You Can't Take It With You* offers a philosophy of life which, in the main, consists of having as much fun as possible while one has the chance to do so. Proceeds from the show went to the Leeds Home for Aged Jews. With Alec's great sensitivity to the text, he encouraged a relaxed and friendly ambience and encouraged a lot of laughter through rehearsals which at one point unintentionally spilled over into the actual performance.

The Pross took the show to Ilkley Playhouse in May where it played to excellent houses for a whole week. It also presented the company with a lesson they would never forget. Thelma Lander, who played Gay Wellington, had a scene where she was completely inebriated and passes out on the sofa. At one performance, however, Miss Lander started to listen to the dialogue and was amazed to discover that she was in a comedy. Finding the situation hilariously funny the actress, with her head buried under a cushion, started to have a fit of the giggles which could not be suppressed. Rosalyn Silverton (Whyman) remembers that one of the eight actors on stage saw the actress's body shaking with laughter and also joined in.

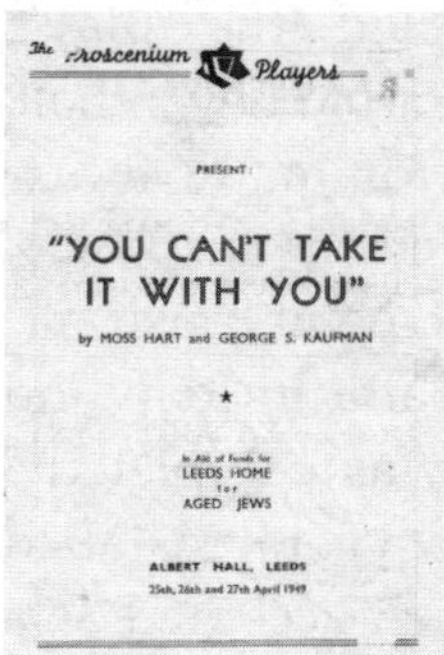

The high spirits became infectious, she recalled. As the scene progressed, the giggling passed to each member of the cast, until all eight thespians were convulsed with laughter. As each one became affected it was not long before the audience, realising what was going on, also joined in.

Rosalyn said: 'I have never known anything like it before or since. They were laughing so much I suddenly pulled myself up short and realised I had to do something to save the situation. So through clenched teeth I said the next line which led to another actor's response and eventually the scene continued.'

After the end of the act, the whole company received a

severe telling off from Pamela Cowan who was waiting in the wings, furious with the whole company. 'What do you think you're doing? How unprofessional', she scolded adding a few choice expletives.

Rosalyn continues: 'This was fine, we needed to be reprimanded. But what Pam didn't realise was there was a microphone in the wings that picked up every word, swear words and all, relaying them to the audience. More laughter, hilarity and embarrassment, it was becoming a real-life farce - I'm so glad Alec wasn't there to witness the fiasco.'

Two young members who constructed the play's impressive setting were Sheila Casimir and Harold Leventhall, who were to work relentlessly backstage for many future productions. Judith Baron recalls being called upon to help, and was given an overall, a tin of paint and a paint brush.

'I spent several days slapping on the paint in Joan and Max Gordon's garage and when the set was completed I remember climbing on board the lorry to help get it installed in the theatre. By this time I still hadn't been accepted as a member, I was sort of 'on approval' - but I had already made friends with Cyril Livingstone and Cecil Korer and they very kindly sponsored me. My application was eventually accepted which was a great honour and a relief.

'When we took the play to Ilkley I was responsible for the music, which meant standing with the arm of the gramophone needle poised over the record to start at the exact point. This was quite a balancing act and I had to be very precise - from then on music became my forte.'

For its first season, the Proscenium Players had produced four successful plays - all hugely well supported. The group had overcome the trials and tribulations that any first season was likely to offer and not only gathered a large, keen and talented group, but also a following of local theatrical intelligentsia, impressed by the professional aims.

Excuse My Apron...
We're Shelling Peas For Drying
The Proposal

One of the aspirations of the group was to donate certain sums for charity; the first season had, after all, been presented under the sponsorship of charitable organisations. The company had now become known as The Pross, an affectionate derivative of the word Proscenium. With packed houses, they had managed to raise quite a considerable sum of money. In fact, in their first season the Proscenium Players had raised the magnificent sum of £1,000 for charity. It was clear to all and sundry that this dynamic amateur stage troupe was here to stay.

However, as productions expanded so did the high standards of the company and therefore the cost of presenting them went through the roof. Many of the charities behind the productions soon objected to the excessive expenditure, as the overhead costs cut drastically into the funds they eventually received.

This gave the group quite a problem. The sponsors seemed to be taking over and dictating how much should be

Above: Cecil Korer and Cyril Livingstone in *Cockpit*, 1950

spent on each production. After a long debate at an Annual General Meeting it was felt that sometime in the future the group should stride out independently. So they proposed a policy of obtaining funding by the acquisition of private patrons and advertisers. Nevertheless, for the time being the Pross decided to go on as they were and to file the new way of funding under 'Plan B.' In any case, they had an ambitious programme planned for the seasons ahead with a long list of plays that appealed to them, including Priestley's little-known drama *Home is Tomorrow*, Elmer Rice's *The Adding Machine*, and Chekhov's *The Seagull*.

The company began its second season with Irwin Shaw's powerful anti-war play, *Bury the Dead*. Set in 'the second year of the war that is to begin tomorrow night' the play told the story of a burial party in the process of digging a mass grave when six dead soldiers of different religions and backgrounds stand up and refuse to lie down again. They question the morality of the politicians who sent them to war and took away their lives needlessly. In an ending that proved to be a real coup de théâtre, the General orders the men of the burial detail to machine gun the soldiers, but they refuse. In a horrific climax he fires the machine gun himself but the dead men simply walk out of the trench and into the audience.

The play had a cast of nearly 30 that included Max Rawnsley, Gerry Riche, Anthony Kristall and Jon Rummelsburg, Myrtle Young and Rosalyn Whyman. It also had nearly 50 patrons and advertisers, which brought in revenue for The Friends of Israel, Histadrut, Social Welfare Fund. On the opening night the play received seven curtain calls although many in the audience thought the play's content was controversial, one critic noting: 'It was not in the best of taste – definitely not for the hyper-sensitive and certainly not for the squeamish.'

Cyril Livingstone recalled the horror that some people felt at seeing the play. 'There was one scene between Vivienne Jacobs as the mother Mrs Dean and Harold Leventhall as her son, who had been badly disfigured with half his face blown away. She kept imploring him to turn his face to her, which he shielded, and when he eventually turned round you saw the ghastly wound. Vivienne started to scream hysterically and simultaneously Alec had this tremendous lighting effect of about five different spotlights hitting the face one after the other. The result was astonishing... quite a few people fainted in the audience.'

As a curtain-raiser, Alec produced Chekhov's satirical one-act play *The Proposal* (or *A Marriage Proposal*) set in a charming eight-foot high box, with two Russian peasants on either side looking in at the action.

Chekhov describes the odd courtship of Lomov who seeks marriage with his neighbour Stepan's daughter Natalya. After he has received permission Lomov is invited into the room but the couple get into an argument about a disputed piece of land and hypochondriac Lomov gets palpitations and a numb leg and leaves the house. Stepan tells his daughter that Lomov was about to propose and at this news Natalya screams to bring him back. He does so and Natalya and Lomov start arguing again bringing on another more violent palpitation. This time father and daughter think Lomov has died. However, he regains consciousness and Stepan almost forces the couple to seal the proposal with a kiss. Immediately after their embrace the couple start to argue again.

With the theme that true love never does run smoothly and Chekhov's observation that marriage is comical, Thelma Lander, Cecil Korer and Cyril Livingstone showed their expertise at comic timing. Cyril recalls Thelma causing havoc during one of the performances. 'Thelma was coming down to the evening performance on the tramcar and going through her script she suddenly decided to change the moves she had been given, without telling Cecil and myself. She thought her first scene would be better played stage right instead of stage left and sitting down instead of standing up. Consequently, Cecil and I both kept turning to her and she'd be in a completely different part of the stage. It was a nightmare and we all dried. When we stormed off the stage and confronted her afterwards she merely replied: 'I meant to tell you, but I forgot. I think it worked better that way, didn't you?'

Mainly as a result of the experience with the over-heated pot dimmers, the Albert Hall had, in the summer recess, acquired a complete make-over and the City Fathers, realising how popular the venue had become as the home of the amateur stage movement decided to improve the facilities. Apart from enlarging the stage area and considerably improving the sound and lighting equipment, much thought had been given to increasing the comfort of

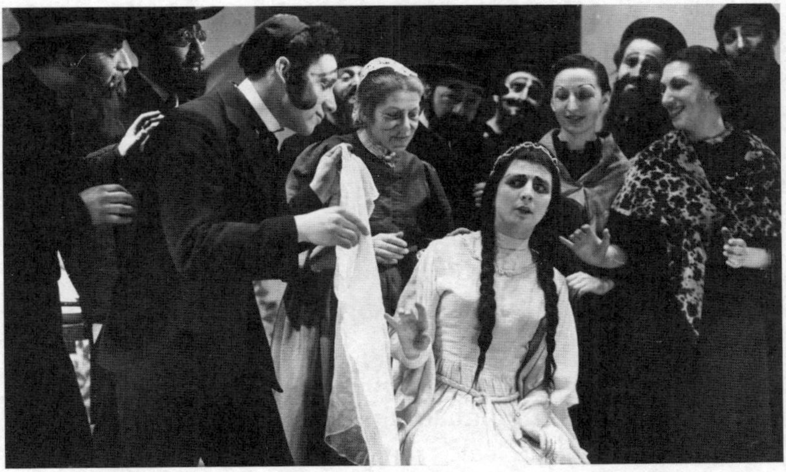

Above: Myrtle Young takes centre stage in a 1950 production of *The Dybbuk*

the players in quite spacious dressing rooms. The theatre had been re-wired and a new switchboard installed in a control room situated at the back of the circle. These improvements now made it possible to hire adequate spotlights and more sophisticated lighting. The auditorium had also been refurbished and the venue had been transformed from a hall into a smart little theatre.

To celebrate the renovation the theatre was named as Leeds Civic Theatre and held an 'Opening Night' on Monday September 25, 1950.

This was in the form of a gala concert and formally opened by the Lord Mayor of Leeds, Alderman F.H.O'Donnell, JP. Among those participating were the Amati String Quartet, conducted by Bernard Armour, the Leeds Magical Society and the Proscenium Players, who presented Thornton Wilder's stylised one-act play, *The Happy Journey*, directed by Nevil H. Silverton.

'This is a story of a journey by car, without a car,' wrote the *YEP* correspondent. 'It runs through countryside with no countryside visible. It has to rely on the imagination of the audience, but particularly on the suggestive actions of the actors. This is a technique in which the Proscenium Players are outstandingly proficient. It was a delight to see them.'

In his opening address the Lord Mayor declared that the theatre had completely justified its existence since its inauguration. It now had 2,000 affiliated members. He made a plea for a high standard in drama. No hackneyed comedies or farces, he said, but something of real worth.

The guest speaker was William Dunn, Secretary of the Birmingham and District Theatre Guild, who said that all cities should give their amateur stage movement a theatre like Leeds Civic. 'They were as essential as public libraries and public baths. I look forward to the time when every city has its own Civic Theatre.' Leeds was one of the first cities to get this honour and it now had a great opportunity of lighting a torch for drama which would shine across the country. This could only be achieved by insisting on nothing but the best.

By this time the Pross had gained a distinctive logo that was used for publicity, on letter headings and posters and, of course, the programme. The emblem represented comedy and tragedy on either side of a flaming torch with the central letters PP in black and white. It was designed by Dorothy Griffins, a young artist who lived with her mother in Moortown.

At this time four plays for future production were being considered. These were Moliere's *The Miser*, Maxwell Anderson's *Winterset*, Clifford Odets' *Golden Boy*, S.Ansky's *The Dybbuk* and Dostoevsky's *Crime and Punishment*.

Fired with renewed energy the company soldiered on and followed *Bury The Dead* with a successful production of

Sean O'Casey's *Juno and the Paycock*. This was notable for a brilliant performance by Cecil Korer as Joxer Daly and a memorable tear-jerking cameo performance by Myrtle Young, as Mrs. Tancred. Vivienne Jacobs, as Juno Boyle, came in for some praise in the local press, with the *Yorkshire Post* critic commending Miss Jacobs on a most moving performance, especially in the final tragic scene. The critic also commented that the group showed admirable enterprise in staging the O'Casey masterpiece ending his review: 'a darling play - a darling play!'

Various businesses in Leeds city centre had volunteered to undertake the booking plan and ticket sales, and these turned out to be mostly jewellery shops. All were located in Briggate, and apart from Waterman's there were Shaffner's and Denton's. Keen theatregoers Margot and Harold Denton, who owned Denton's, were to become loyal friends of the group. They offered to take on the task of running the box office regularly in the years ahead and did an admirable job. They handled a time-consuming assignment with courtesy and cool expertise and helped to promote the professional image of the Players.

The Pross also decided to create the role of president and one of the first to be appointed was Dr. Harry Edelston, with Gertrude Rosenthal vice-president. Gertrude was a leading figure in the community, helping to raise vital funds for the recently formed State of Israel.

Gertrude had been appointed chairman of Leeds Women's Zionist Council and was a member of the Hon Officers of the Women's Zionist Federation of Great Britain and Ireland. Many years later she was to become The Pross' president and remained the only woman ever to be given this honour. Others to take on the mantle of president included local business and professional men Charles Sumrie, John Wood, Raymond Ellis, Harold Lander, Jack

Above: Bridget Boland's play *Cockpit* was about the fall-out from World War II

Barnett, Leslie Cohen, Michael Kent, Harry Hurst, Lionel Poyser, Bernard Sandler, Julian Goldberg, David Stross, Dr. Harold Taylor, and Alec Baron.

Money raised by the Pross' next production - Bridget Boland's *Cockpit* - went to the WIZO Baby Home in Jerusalem. The play, presented week commencing February 20, 1950, was about the thousands of displaced persons and freed concentration camp prisoners of all nationalities in Germany just after World War Two. A large theatre had been taken over as a sorting place and a British officer and his blunt Yorkshire sergeant were struggling to keep some kind of order. This production was again directed by the ubiquitous Alec Baron, who used the whole theatre as a platform for the play, with the audience as part of the bulk of the poor unfortunates being processed. This was total theatre at its best, which Alec loved to do, and the cast once again rose to the occasion. It was hailed as a triumph by the press with the *Yorkshire Evening Post* writing: 'With the greatest respect for other amateur directors we wish Mr. Baron would give all of them tickets for his productions.'

A message from the Pross president, Dr. Harry Edelston said *Cockpit* was a tragic play, but one of high purpose and significance with a message very appropriate to the times. 'In keeping with the group's tradition it is not the sort of play to be given in the commercial theatre for in content and presentation it is distinctly unusual, offering a challenge to both the producer and the actors.' WIZO Council chairman Gertrude Rosenthal thought the group was once again fulfilling its obligations to the Jewish community in helping towards so worthy an objective.

Joan Gordon recalls that her late husband Max was cast in the play. 'He had already been in *Bury the Dead*, which had the grimmest of themes. Max played one of the six dead soldiers who refused to be buried. I could barely watch him; the theme sent long shivers down my spine. However, in *Cockpit* he played Bauer, a German stage manager. Alec had spilled the action into the auditorium and Max had to climb an exceptionally tall ladder up towards the roof. I found watching this nerve-wracking and viewed his acrobatics through my fingers which were placed firmly across my face.'

Rosalyn Silverton (nee Whyman) said that for bringing out the finer points and subtleties of a play Alec could not be beaten. 'I had a scene with Jacqui Steinberg where we were two refugees fighting over a pan. It started off where we all slowly arose from the floor, on which we had been sleeping. During an early rehearsal Alec stopped the run through and said: "Just a minute, how many of you have ever slept on a floor before? Because believe me if you had you just wouldn't get up like that". He then spent the rest of the rehearsal showing us the correct way to perform this feat, which turned our rehearsal into a mini workshop. I have never forgotten that lesson. Alec was amazing for getting the actor to think deeply about motivation and purpose; he was a master director and a fine stickler for detail.'

Why Do You Always Answer A Question With A Question?

They Came To Leeds

During these early days, potboilers for commercial gain were certainly not on the Proscenium agenda. Anything deemed remotely popular was frowned upon by the committee. This was a policy that was upheld for many years and, in some ways, was responsible for gaining the group a reputation for being deeply intellectual and 'arty.'

In the early 1950's the amateur stage movement in Leeds had expanded and increased in popularity. The fine new facilities for both rehearsal and presentation had helped to attract larger audiences and new groups were to be seen strutting their stuff on the boards of Leeds Civic Theatre. The Leeds Arts Centre had formed in 1945 and was flourishing; the Leeds Children's Theatre was still going strong since being founded in 1935; and there was quite a batch of successful drama groups, including Leeds Art Theatre, the Cosmopolitans and the Montague Burton Players. All these groups aimed for a higher standard of production but tended to stick with entertainments that proved to be popular 'box office' with the Leeds theatre-going public. The Proscenium Players, however, stuck to their guns and continued to present plays not usually seen on the amateur stage.

Leeds was a flourishing theatrical city with a cultural scenario second to none. It had the Theatre Royal, home to Harry Hanson's famous Court Players, as well as producing memorable pantomimes. Leeds Empire was home to variety and music hall and attracted big names like Sophie Tucker and Billy Eckstein. It will forever be associated with Frankie Vaughan who, as Frank Ableson, was discovered appearing in a 1949 University Rag Revue, directed by Alec Baron.

Leeds City Varieties Music Hall continued a long tradition of vaudeville and striptease, and the Leeds Grand Theatre managed to attract the best in professional entertainment by staging West End plays and new productions 'trying out' in the provinces before sailing into Town. It was also home to touring London musicals that had been transported from Broadway. The era of Ivor Novello extravaganzas at Drury Lane was coming to an end, and modern musicals had suddenly become widely popular after Rodgers and Hammerstein's groundbreaking 1943 production of *Oklahoma!*

Flushed with success after his musical *Salad Days*, composer Sandy Wilson decided that Leeds should premiere his follow-up musical *Free as Air* and Noel Coward had the same idea when he premiered *After the Ball*, his musical adapted from Oscar Wilde's *Lady Windermere's Fan*. Theatrical giants like Laurence Olivier, Sybil Thorndike, Marie Lohr, Beatrice Lillie, Gladys Cooper and Joyce Grenfell would choose to appear at Leeds Grand Theatre. Leeds theatre was doing well; it seemed the entire world and his wife were flocking to this Yorkshire city to enjoy live entertainment at a very high level.

Above: *Lady Precious Stream* was an ambitious end to the second season

S. Hsiung's *Lady Precious Stream* was the play chosen to bring the highly successful second Pross season to a close in April 1950. Four full-length plays had been presented, each one selected solely on the basis of quality and not box-office considerations. Despite the relatively short existence of the group, their prestige stood high with public, press and critics. *Lady Precious Stream* was directed by Alec, whose innovative production values continued to help raise the group's profile. Alec performed this charming piece in the nearest he could get to a genuine Chinese-style setting, presenting it on an empty stage with only a silver birch tree, which changed colour as the scenes progressed. The group hired lavish and elaborate costumes from BBC TV and a cast of nearly 40 actors truly excelled themselves. The capacity audiences loved the show and the group was invited by Leeds City Council to tour the production around the parks during the summer-break, playing the piece in a specially constructed Chinese-style portable theatre.

Joan Gordon recalls: 'We had two actors playing removal

men and they had to sit on stage throughout pretending to cat-nap. It was a very warm summer's day and at one performance one of the actors, Montague Quate, was so relaxed he slept right through the entire scene and nearly fell off his perch. The audience loved it and thought it was part of the plot.'

One of the aims of the Proscenium Players was the presentation of at least one Jewish play of quality a season. But Jewish plays of substance were hard to find. The group had long considered doing the great Jewish classical play *The Dybbuk* but it had a cast of nearly 50, needed several sets, required a special style of acting and would cost a heap of money to stage. It was a massive venture and the committee felt that this should be placed on the back-burner to be reflected upon for production at a later date.

Times were changing, however, and with the recent formation of the State of Israel, the Jewish people now had a national homeland and Israel also possessed its very own army with which to defend itself.

Alec Baron felt the time was right to look for a play that would reflect the conception of not having to shy away when anti-Semitism reared its ugly head, but to fight back. After searching in vain for a play that was based on this concept he decided to write one himself with these ideals intact, and arranged a meeting with Leeds Jewish historian Louis Saipe. Together they researched incidents from the turn of the century when Leeds immigrant Jews fought back against persecution and anti-Semitism. Louis supplied many historical details that gave Alec the motivation and inspiration to turn them into a play, which they called *They Came to Leeds*.

The story, set in the late 1880's, told of life in a district of Leeds known as The Leylands, and illustrated the influx of Jews into the city. In particular it depicted groups of anti-

Semitic gangs of youths from Hunslet who continually harassed the recently-arrived Jewish immigrants while the police did nothing to stop them. It also included a piece of well known history. To combat the attacks on Jewish funerals by hooligans, a small group of Jewish lads decided to band together to counter-attack and defend the processions.

The play was an outstanding success and, due to popular demand, had to be performed on four separate occasions. Cyril Livingstone, as well as featuring in a prominent character part, produced authentic set designs with the help of local artist Ronald Lipman.

A new orchestra was formed because Alec had persuaded the Pross committee to structure its own band of musicians and had advertised in the local press. As a result the ELJOS Orchestra (Leeds Jewish Orchestral Society) was launched under the direction of Louis Marks and its first 'gig' was in the orchestra pit. Its leader was Norbert Fox and the orchestra delighted audiences with plaintive Jewish folk melodies and Israeli national dances, which added considerably to the show's ambience. Alec had written some of the incidental music and Arnold Morris arranged the pieces for the orchestra. The ELJOS later branched out independently but the relationship with the Proscenium Players remained a happy one.

The first performance in the week commencing October 23, 1950, was a revelation. The play proved to be not only poignant but also very humorous with every Jewish epigram and bit of stage business being greeted with warmth and nostalgia by a delighted audience. The mere mention of 'Camp Road' or 'salt herrings in a barrel' brought ripples of laughter throughout the theatre. Many of the audiences were actually witnessing a facsimile of their lives and that of their own parents and grandparents upon the

Left: Jon Rumney, Cyril Livingstone and Jennie Stratton in *They Came To Leeds.* It proved to be a massive success, written by Alec Baron and historian Louis Saipe

Leeds Civic Theatre stage. The setting was a faithful one and a sentimental reproduction of Avrom Ber's Yard in Bridge Street. Avrom Ber was a backyard that was well known as a meeting place and it was named after Louis Saipe's grandfather. The play also showed how the Francis Street Synagogue was founded and the style of playing leaned towards the style of Yiddish Theatre. Cecil Korer as Yaffe, the cynical pocket philosopher tailor, sitting cross-legged on a table sewing his garments, stopped the show every night. The play was full of Jewish jokes - 'Why do you always answer a question with a question?' 'Why not?' And the entrance of Cyril Livingstone and Jennie Stratton as two Russian immigrants on a wheelbarrow clutching their few belongings brought the house down.

Cecil recalled the impact the play had on the community. 'It hit the city like a bombshell and packed in audiences every night. In fact, the demand for tickets became so great that we had waiting lists for cancellations. I remember my late mother was out shopping and a woman to whom she hadn't spoken for years approached her and began enquiring as to the family's health. After some minutes of going through the whole dynasty the woman suddenly enquired if my mother could get her and her husband tickets for the show.'

Cecil loved playing the part of Yaffe, the tailor, but not without a certain amount of criticism from the character's creator Alec Baron, who objected at Cecil playing for laughs. 'At rehearsals Alec kept telling me that it was not being played as he had envisaged. After the final dress rehearsal he took me home in his car and informed me in no uncertain way that he was not happy with my interpretation of the character.

'He saw Yaffe as a sort of heavy, serious thinker who continually comments about life and people. I saw him more as a light-hearted, comical and philosophical character. Nevertheless, I stuck to my guns and concentrated in bringing out the comedy aspect, and I'm glad to say my interpretation caused roars of laughter.'

Nowhere Is There A Place For Me
The Dybbuk

The Society hit a snag before opening night and made the national newspapers the day after. This was because of a dispute with Leeds City Council. Eight hours before the curtain went up on the opening night of *They Came To Leeds*, the Pross was told by Irene Clayden, chairman of the Leeds Civic Theatre sub-committee, that the ELJOS orchestra must be whittled down to 11 players until after 9pm, eliminating all brass and percussion instruments. The reason was that the theatre was situated right next door to Leeds Technical School and evening class students were being disturbed by the sound of music. When the classes finished at 9pm the musicians were then allowed back into the orchestra pit to rejoin the rest of the orchestra.

'Students cannot be expected to study with the crash of cymbals in the background,' a corporation spokesperson said. 'Violins and piano, yes, but percussion and brass, certainly not!'

From a financial aspect the play proved to be the greatest success the group had ever known and hurtled the

Above: The enormous demands of *The Dybbuk* did not faze the Pross

Proscenium Players' third season off to a stupendous start. With money in the bank, a huge theatrical following and a reputation that was as high as Leeds Town Hall the Proscenium Players at last felt they were able to tackle the demands of *The Dybbuk*.

It was to be the most costly and prestigious production the group had ever staged as Alec Baron demanded four sets to be built in a distorted, impressionistic way, without right angles and painted in a specific expressionistic style. Enquiries were made locally for the right builders for such a mammoth task, but to no avail. The committee decided to splash out and the commission was eventually given to a top-rate firm of theatrical scene builders in London called Brunskill and Loveday. They produced the finest sets ever to be seen at the Leeds Civic Theatre and the production was hailed as a minor masterpiece of staging and execution.

With a cast of over 40 players Alec took an extended rehearsal period of four months. The style of acting had to be developed and one of the first tasks was to plunge the entire company into studying a way of life and the fundamental principles that the Chasidic movement adopted.

The play followed the philosophy of Chasidism which addressed itself to those Jews who were left spiritually impoverished by the Chmielnicki Massacres. At the centre of each Chasidic community was a leader known as The Tzaddik, who was believed to work miracles and act as a channel for divine energy to flow into the human race. The Movement also believed in the ability of the soul of a dead person to enter into that of another living person. It showed also that rabbis could work miracles and even recall the dead to give evidence against the living.

When news broke that the group was to perform the play Alec was approached by the notable Leeds artist Jacob Kramer, whom he had known for many years and whose work included ultra-orthodox Jewish subjects. Kramer's haunting painting *Day of Atonement* is a celebrated work that still hangs in Leeds Art Gallery. Kramer, who was born in 1892, came to Leeds from Russia with his parents in 1900. His mother was a trained singer and his father was an artist but the family lived in reduced circumstances. Kramer was something of a local celebrity but lived in utter poverty and alcoholism all his adult life. He produced poor quality portraits of local figures just to pay for his drinks.

Kramer informed Alec that it had always been one of his ambitions to design the sets for *The Dybbuk*. He requested permission to go ahead and submit his ideas and a script was immediately delivered to him. Unfortunately, Kramer was now very much under the influence of alcohol and as the date of the show grew nearer and nearer he failed to deliver the designs. After a few abortive attempts to pin him down which involved Alec going round to his lodgings and pleading with him to submit his designs the group decided to go ahead without Kramer's contribution and Cyril

Livingstone stepped into the breach and designed the sets. His drawings were then sent off to London. Cyril's designs proved to be inspirational and haunting and were one of the highlights of a production that is still remembered today.

Cyril said: 'Because Kramer had let us down time was pressing and Alec was due to go away on holiday. Before he went he asked me to do the set designs. All I had to go on was a description early on in the play that the walls of the two synagogues should look as if they were weeping.'

The Dybbuk turned out to be the pinnacle of Alec's theatrical work. The production, staged week commencing December 18, 1950, was hailed as the greatest piece of drama to be seen on the Leeds Civic Theatre stage. The play had not been seen in Leeds since 1925 and the community flocked to the Civic Theatre to see it. Individual performances were outstanding, particularly Myrtle Young as Leah, the possessed bride, and Myer Steinberg as Rabbi Azrael. The climactic scene of the exorcism was awesome and for some theatregoers quite overpowering.

David Stross played Channon and Jennie Stratton played Frade, Leah's grandmother. Many members of the Leeds Jewish community were recruited to play small character parts including Nevil Ziff, Sydney Gordon, David Abel, Barbara Niman, Walter Waldenberg, Irving Newman, Irma Rowlands and Isadore Fisch. Mother and daughter Minnie and Leila Tagger also made an appearance.

Judith Baron remembered that 1950s state-of-the-art technology was very much in evidence during this production. 'As well as working a follow-spot I had to organise the music from the projection box at the back of the theatre,' she says. 'This was the first time that had been attempted because, previously, music had been executed from the side of the stage.'

Writing in the show's programme Mark Labovitch, who

Above: Myer Steinberg in Ansky's *The Dybbuk,* Alec Baron's pinnacle of success
Below: Myrtle Young and Jennie Stratton in the same 1950 production

was the president of Leeds Jewish Representative Council, commented: 'It is befitting for Ansky's great classic that all proceeds are to be donated to the Blue and White Bazaar funds. Once again, we are indebted to the Proscenium Players for their magnificent achievement in presenting such a play to Leeds. It is worthy to note that two young bodies of different interests can unite for a common cause - surely a lesson for all of us in these uncertain times.'

Above: Moliere's *The Miser* met with only limited success in 1951

The Pross also enlisted the Junior Organisation for Leeds Jewish Charities in organising the brochure and obtaining donations, extra patrons and advertisers to fill the coffers to pay for this expensive production.

Mr Labovitch remarked: 'These young workers realising their great opportunity for service to the community have not spared themselves in their efforts towards raising funds for all charitable causes in this city. It is even more gratifying to note that apart from the financial aspect so many of them feel a sense of responsibility towards the wider issues of communal work.'

Shortly after the production was staged at Leeds Civic Theatre the company received an invitation to repeat the show in Germany. Cyril said: 'We were asked to take the production to an amateur drama festival and they would pay all expenses for the whole production team and find accommodation for us all. We were very excited about the invitation but, when the suggestion was discussed at committee, Myrtle Young refused to go. There was still a lot of ill feeling towards the country and Myrtle stood fast and said there would be no way that she would visit Germany. As she was a staunch committee member, as well as a respected member of the group, and, of course, playing the leading role, we declined the offer.'

It was a difficult task to follow the artistic success of *The Dybbuk* but the Players had just the right play up their sleeve and, in the week commencing February 19, 1951, decided on a production of Moliere's *The Miser* in an adaptation by Miles Malleson.

To date, Alec had directed every play since the group's formation. He decided that it was time to sit back a little and take a rest. His wife Judith had presented him with the first of their four children and Alec wanted to spend some quality time with his new, extended family. The reins were therefore handed over to Cyril Livingstone who had long been directing from the sidelines and wanted to take full charge of direction.

The play proved to be a moderate success, however, with one or two cool reviews. The *Yorkshire Post* theatre critic noted that it lacked pace and polish. Gerry Riche, nevertheless, as Jacques, Harpagon's servant, came in for some praise. 'An outstanding example of playing a small part so that it remains in the memory,' noted the *Yorkshire Evening News*.

The next production was to be Aristophanes' *Lysistrata* in an adaptation by Ewan McColl, originally done for Joan Littlewood's Theatre Workshop. It saw the quick return of Alec, who now wanted to direct alternate productions. With this show the group broke with tradition and actually opened at the Harrogate Festival of Drama in the Royal Hall on October 22, 1951. The adjudicator called it 'a masterpiece of presentation,' and went on to say that it had one of the highest standards of execution he had ever witnessed in the amateur theatre.

Two days later the production sailed triumphantly into the Leeds Civic Theatre from October 24 – November 3, 1951. On the Wednesday night performance the players received some heckling from the gallery. Theatregoers were astonished when a love scene between Rosalyn Whyman and Cyril Livingstone was interrupted by calls and loud comments from a group of young schoolboys. One boy continued to call down to the stage and a theatre official was requested to investigate. Some minutes later the offending schoolboys were escorted out of the theatre.

The incident did not go unnoticed in the press. Headlines the following day claimed that: 'Boy Barrackers at Greek Play Sought in Leeds.' Writing in the *Yorkshire Post* about the play, Ernest Bradbury said that Alec had made clever use of the stage by allowing his players to come down into the audience. He managed to mass his forces with great skill.

The Pross was not above creating a bit of drama off stage as well as on, and in 1952, the group appeared at Leeds County Court. The group had hired John Williams, a theatrical scenery builder from Bushey, Hertfordshire, to build the scenery for *Lysistrata* at a cost of £77. After the scenery had been delivered, however, it was discovered that the pillars were unstable, transparent and would not support properly. A telegram for Mr. Williams to come to Leeds to rectify the faults was sent immediately.

Mr. Williams said in court that he travelled to Leeds and arrived about three hours before the dress rehearsal. Although he offered to rectify matters Alec Baron would not allow him to do so. Four of the wings had already started to

Above: Myer Steinberg as the Magistrate in Ewan McColl's *Lysistrata*, 1951

warp and some of the joints were coming apart. This, he felt, had occurred during the scenery's transit as the timber used was unseasoned.

The builder claimed that he could have fixed matters in time for the first performance but Alec thought that this could not be done.

Isadore Fisch, solicitor and member of the group who was acting for the Pross, said that only part of the scenery supplied by Mr. Williams had been used in the production and the hessian that simulated stonework was of poor quality and the cause of some of the problems.

Mr. Williams was demanding the balance of the account amounting to £24.10s, which had been withheld when the bill had been paid. The Pross counter-claimed for the repayment by Mr. Williams of £23.10s. A sum of £1 was therefore handed over.

Following this, the group staged the first amateur

Above: Rosalyn Whyman, centre, was rudely interrupted in *Lysistrata*

production in Britain of Arthur Miller's classic drama *All My Sons*, during the week commencing December 17, 1951. The group had waited three years for permission to present this play and it offered fine opportunities to the company, particularly Myer Steinberg who played Joe Keller and Myrtle Young who played his wife Kate. It was directed by Alec Baron and Cyril Livingstone. Cyril had by this time become an invaluable member of the company, not only acting as co-director and designing the sets but also playing leading roles.

In the cast was a young actress, Jacqueline Steinberg, who played the part of Lydia Luby. Jacqui was to play many character parts with the company and later to marry Harry Hurst, a stalwart of the group both in administrative and technical duties.

Yes, I Can Be Very Cruel... I Have Been Taught By Masters
The Heiress

As well as assembling a magnificent portfolio of plays, the Pross had managed to motivate quite a few of its actors into turning professional. Most notably Gerry Riche, a character actor who had scored quite a hit with his performance of the Paycock 'Captain' Jack Boyle in *Juno and the Paycock*.

Gerry turned to broadcasting and gained much success in the Monday night series *We're not Stopping* and *Variety Fanfare*. Pamela Cowan also turned professional and on her 21st birthday took a deep breath and went into the office of a hard-to-impress London agent. In a dazzling audition she won him over and was informed that she would make her first professional stage appearance at Stockport. Pam had made a hit with her work in the Leeds University Rag Revue at Leeds Empire that first introduced Frankie Vaughan. Consequently she featured in quite a lot of radio work and kept popping up on TV. She featured in early episodes of the BBC situation comedy *The Good Life* and was a hairdresser in Jack Rosenthal's TV play *Barmitzvah Boy*.

In February 1952, the Players presented one of their most enjoyable and popular productions, John Van Druten's *I Remember Mama*. The cast of 24 had to learn to speak American with a Norwegian accent, which they achieved by listening to recordings. To reach the authentic lilt Alec insisted that even the backstage staff learn the accent as well and insisted every member of the company spoke in this way throughout the rehearsal period. That this was accomplished was confirmed by a Norwegian couple who happened to be visiting Leeds that week and decided to see the play. They were astounded with the results and enquired how the group had managed to get together such a large cast of Norwegian actors.

Zelda Black, now one of the group's leading character actresses, gave a brilliant performance as Mama, and Cecil Korer as Uncle Chris ensured that in his deathbed scene there was not a dry eye in the house.

For their next production Alec Baron decided to take a rest and handed over the mantle of director to Cyril. The committee was keen to present Ruth and August Goetz's *The Heiress*. This was the last play of the fourth season and the committee felt that some attempt at a popular play was justified. Alec was against the move and thought the play not in keeping with the Constitution as it tipped its hat to the commercial theatre. Nevertheless, the high costs of the last few productions had eaten away some of the profits made from *They Came to Leeds* and it was felt that this production would rescue them from their sadly depleted finances.

During the last three years, the Proscenium Players had raised over £4,000 for charity and presented 18 plays not normally staged in the provinces. *The Heiress* had received a highly successful production in London's West End with Peggy Ashcroft and Ralph Richardson and it was felt that the play's enormous popularity would bring in a new audience and help fill the group's coffers. Based on a Henry James novel it had been adapted by Ruth and Augustus Goetz.

Cyril went all out to make this tale of Washington Square 1850 come to life and immediately hired the London production's beautiful and lavish costumes. Rosalyn Whyman as the repressed heiress Catherine Sloper, wore the costumes made for Peggy Ashcroft and had eight changes of gowns to make during the running of the show. The magnificent outfits were also in near pristine condition having been exclusively worn only by professional actors; and their name tags were still sewn into the lining. The Pross' leading actors felt very grand getting into clothes with the names of Ralph Richardson and Peggy Ashcroft's resting comfortably in the nape of their necks.

The imposing antique furniture was hired from Kirkstall's Abbey House Museum and the solid period set designed and built by Leeds Civic Theatre employee Fred Mower. It came as no surprise that apart from a handful of star performances, notably Cyril Livingstone as Dr. Soper and Rosalyn Whyman as his daughter, the local press mentioned nearly all the back-stage technical staff for their dedication and hard work, including Nevil Silverton who created some beautifully atmospheric lighting. The play was both an artistic success and a financial one. The Players were back in the bank manager's good books.

Rosalyn Silverton (Whyman) recalls being very excited when she was cast as Catherine. 'The West End production was a tremendous success, so I felt I had been given a terrific part to play. Any role that requires a transformation of character offers a huge challenge to an actress. I knuckled down and learned the part very quickly, as we all were encouraged to do. I got a special thrill when the wonderful

Above: Zelda Black, Rosalyn Whyman and Gerald Coleman in *The Heiress*, 1952

costumes arrived from London. I had already rehearsed with an enormous hoop around me and recall being taken to somebody's house where there was a French-window. We practiced many times going in and out so that handling the dresses looked elegant and natural. I remember Myer Steinberg coming into my dressing room at the dress rehearsal and looking into the mirror over my shoulder as I was applying my make-up. 'Hmm, something wrong there, Roz, you look too pretty.' I immediately got hold of the wig I was to wear with the severe centre parting, put it on my head and turned round to face him. 'Oh, that's alright then,' he said and edged out of the room.

Cyril said: 'This was definitely one of my favourite productions. It was well cast, had a strong story to tell and looked fantastic. The set received applause every night and on the whole it was a very happy production in which to be involved.'

After the summer recess, the Players returned to action once again and, with batteries re-charged plus an expanding audience and membership, they opened the 1952-53 season with Alec Baron once again at the helm directing Moliere's *Tartuffe*.

Alec, however, was not too happy with the outcome due to the fact that the leading actor could not cope with the demands of the part during the rehearsal period and had to drop out. His successor had difficulty learning the lines, which ruined any finesse the director had hoped for. However the *Yorkshire Evening Post* critic felt the play maintained a professional touch throughout, both in its presentation and acting, and urged theatregoers to see the production as it was near to the perfection of Miles Malleson's original as was likely to be seen on any amateur stage.

With this season the Players had reached the decision to embark upon a new method of financial administration. This related to the policy that had been discussed openly at the AGM between the first and second season. Instead of restricting the sponsorship of each play to one charitable organisation, the Players themselves would now undertake the responsibility for backing each production. At the end of the season any financial surplus would be distributed amongst as many charitable organisations as was practicable. To date having one financial sponsor certainly had relieved the group of many financial worries and anxieties and they had no delusions about the burdens they would now shoulder. It was felt that the new method would eventually give them greater freedom to expand and to increase their artistic activities, to the ultimate advantage both of their creative work and the distribution of profits to local charities.

The search for avant-garde and unusual plays for future productions continued and the committee advertised for public assistance.

Amongst the plays they were looking for were H. Berger's *The Deluge,* H. Goldfaden's *The Witch,* Shalom Aleichem's *200,000,* A. Zeitlin's *Wise Men of Chelm* and Peretz Hirshbein's *The Haunted Inn.* One of the plays they were really keen to acquire was Shalom Asch's *The God of Vengeance.* The only copy of the play in the country was in the possession of the British Museum, and the committee set out to obtain a duplicated copy. However, when it eventually arrived the play proved to be disappointing.

The next production, held week commencing February 16, 1953, was to be Gerhart Hauptmann's *Lonely Lives* (Einsame Menschen). This was again directed by Alec Baron, who had great admiration for the play but knew in his heart that it would not attract large audiences.

The opening night marked the group's 100th performance and the company received many messages of congratulations from past players, as well as members of the audience and press representatives and patrons. Marjorie Saunders designed a magnificent set that drew huge applause from the opening-night audience and Cyril Livingstone gave an excellent performance as Dr Vockerat.

It was thought that the production was possibly the British premiere of the play. Enquiries made to the Leeds University drama department brought back a response that this was not so, as it was recorded that it had been staged in the country some time before World War One!

Making his debut in this production, as the artist Braun, was Richard Courtnay. Richard was to play in several future productions, eventually relocating to Canada where he became a Professor of Drama and the author of some 30 text books dealing with drama and the theatre. In a preface for one of these books, Richard acknowledged how much he had learned from working with Alec and the Proscenium Players.

Above: The Proscenium Players' 1953 production of Hauptmann's *Lonely Lives*

The Pross chose a Romeo and Juliet story for their next show, week commencing April 20, 1953. Set in the East End of London during the years of the Second World War, Yvonne Mitchell's play about inter-marriage *The Same Sky* had received a moderate success on the West End stage and the Proscenium committee thought the play, dealing with a pair of star-crossed lovers from different faiths, worked very well as a comedy, tragedy and an indictment on human intolerance. It also had a strong Jewish theme which appealed to the group.

Cyril Livingstone was now firmly in the director's seat, and Rosalyn Whyman, as Esther Brodsky, the Jewish girl who falls in love with a Gentile, made quite an impression. She particularly excelled in the scene where she receives a telegram informing her of her lover's death in the armed forces. However, Rosalyn's emotional distress caused one member of the audience to storm down to the foot of the stage and call out 'It serves you b----y well right!' as he marched smartly out of the theatre. Audience participation had truly arrived.

You Shall Have The Support And Applause Of My Newspapers
Major Barbara

Making my own debut with the group in 1953 was a tremendous thrill. After my unsuccessful audition for Manny in *The Same Sky* I was offered a lovely vignette in The *Relapse* (or *Virtue in Danger*) directed by Alec. The production welcomed the return to Leeds of actor Jon Rumney who had been serving with the army in Germany and, in fact, was still there ten days before the opening night. He had been sent a script and studied the part over there.

Cyril Livingstone made a fine job of Sir Novelty Fashion, the newly created Lord Foppington, and newcomer Colin Morton, a former RADA student, played Young Fashion, his brother, in dashing style. The show, opening week commencing December 14, 1953, turned out to be a winner and gained the group more publicity than it had ever had before, mainly due to excellent acting throughout, not only in the leading parts but in the smaller character parts as well. It was beautifully costumed and had some fine sets.

Above: Author John Fisher's Pross debut was in *The Relapse* - aka *Virtue In Danger*

Although Richard Courtney was given the opportunity to try his hand at directing the next production, Bernard Shaw's classic *Major Barbara*, presented week commencing December 14, 1953, he handed over to Alec three weeks into rehearsal. Richard had been cast as Andrew Undershaft, but found difficulty in juggling the part as well as directing.

I received a phone call from Alec one evening. Cecil Korer, who had been cast as Peter Shirley, had to drop out because of illness and I was invited to take over. 'It's a sizeable character role and you appear in Act Two in the Salvation Army yard scene ... it's a smashing part,' he said.

Playing my first major role at the age of 16 years was an auspicious occasion and, although I was certainly the youngest on board, I felt no age barrier existed in the group. I was fortunate to forge friendships that lasted all my life.

It was evident that the group had a very strong technical team; one man in particular was outstanding. Harry Hurst, who headed stage management, was perhaps the best production manager the Pross ever had. Charming, erudite and a perfectionist he steered the group through many stormy technical problems. His presence backstage had a calming influence and his professionalism was much admired.

Major Barbara proved to be a huge artistic hit. The Salvation Army scene stopped the show, as did Colin Morton, as Bill Walker. Jacqueline Heyward made a brilliant Barbara and the production attracted many new admirers.

Angus Turner, writing in the *YEP*, wrote: 'The production was a fine one and without qualification I make the Salvation Army scene one of the finest things seen on the amateur stage for a long time.' Writing again in his *Amateur Stage* column later in the week, Mr. Turner wrote that when he took over as drama critic for the *YEP* he was warned never to rave about any one production or player - he would always live to regret it. However, Mr. Turner maintained that the impact of the Salvation Army scene would stay with him for a long time.

He kindly gave me my first review: 'Sixteen-year-old John Fisher gave a polished performance ...' but Alec was furious; he didn't want anyone to know my age and held a small investigation as to who 'leaked' the news to the papers. It was all terribly serious and intense but, from my point of view, hugely enjoyable. Mr. Turner was an erudite and kindly critic and gave the Pross continued support for quite a few seasons.

The committee chose an old Unity Theatre favourite, Clifford Odets' *Awake and Sing* for their spring 1954 production. Eddie Malkin was invited to be guest director and he assembled a strong cast with Rosalyn Whyman as Hennie Berger, Anita Silverton as Bessie Berger, and Ron Lipman as the grandfather. The play told of the problems of a Jewish family living in a Bronx tenement during the time of the Depression. It had a bitterly accurate characterisation from Colin Morton as Moe Axelrod, a war-torn neurotic. Colin was to leave the group shortly afterwards. His participation in the last three productions had given him the taste for the real thing and he went into professional repertory theatre. We shared a dressing room and he advised me to apply for drama school; he was very encouraging. So was Cyril Livingstone who was also in demand playing selected weeks with the Court Players, in Leeds, Keighley and Halifax.

Emlyn Williams' semi-autobiographical play *The Corn is Green* followed in the week commencing April 26, 1954. At its core the play dealt with Miss Moffatt, a formidable schoolteacher working in a small poverty-stricken coal-mining town, who tutors an illiterate teenager, the son of a Welsh miner, who eventually graduates with honours and goes to Oxford. The play had two exceptional performances, one from Myrtle Young as Miss Moffatt, and the other from newcomer Michael Page as her student Morgan Evans. During the rehearsal period the committee discovered that the original Miss Moffat was still alive and residing in Wales. A letter was despatched inviting her to attend a performance and she accepted. It was quite strange knowing that the real Miss Moffat was sitting there watching herself depicted on stage.

This was the first time I was told I had a good singing voice. I played the tiny role of Old Tom and was also placed in the choir of Welsh singers who sang live from the wings. Nevil Silverton, who did the lighting, was also choirmaster and led us in the singing of two Welsh pieces. One evening at rehearsal, Nevil said someone was singing flat and he strolled around the group to find the culprit. Thankfully, it wasn't me, because he said afterwards: 'John, you have a really beautiful singing voice; you should cultivate that gift.'

Not one to be first off the mark, I was to take his advice some 50 years later when I joined the Potato Room Players, the resident musical drama company at Leeds City Varieties. I decided to take singing lessons from teacher Muriel Smith who lived on Street Lane. She coached me through 'I Love to Cry at Weddings' from *Sweet Charity*, 'Everybody Ought to Have a Maid' from *A Funny Thing Happened on the Way to the Forum*, 'Stiff Upper Lip' from *Crazy for You* and through the 'Contract Scene' from *Gigi*, one of the most difficult musical numbers ever written, I'll be bound.

For the October 1954 production, and to start the new season, the group settled on a reprise of *They Came to Leeds*. Presented by public demand it ran for two weeks and it was interesting to see that this time around 50 per cent of the audience was non-Jewish. The play again met with a healthy response. Rosalyn Whyman once more played Rosie and complained that with each revival the bride was getting older, and the bridegrooms were getting younger. This time I became her husband-to-be Jack Simon and had the task of standing on a soap box in order to kiss my bride!

Cecil Korer reprised the role of Yaffe the tailor; and had us all in stitches in the wedding scene, making risqué comments in whispered asides as we stood centre stage under the canopy.

In 1955, the group staged an exceptionally moving production of Tennessee Williams' *The Glass Menagerie*, directed by Cyril Livingstone, who also played the role of Jim O'Connor, the gentleman caller. Williams' lovely drama gave four actors amazing parts to play. Rosalyn Whyman particularly scored with her sensitive and accomplished portrayal of the daughter Laura. The production had a cinematic effect and the lighting, designed by Nevil Silverton, became an important feature and had nearly 50 lighting cues. Every time the father's name was mentioned his on-stage picture lit up and the fade-in fade-out effect of the scenes was slickly handled. As Southern belle Amanda Wingfield, Sadie Cornick, an accomplished elocution and drama teacher and the Players' honourable secretary, gave a memorable performance.

Rosalyn recalled the excitement of the first night. 'There was this moment in the interval when someone rushed backstage to say the critic from the *Yorkshire Evening Post* was in raptures about the production. He not only phoned the paper to reserve more space than usual for his review

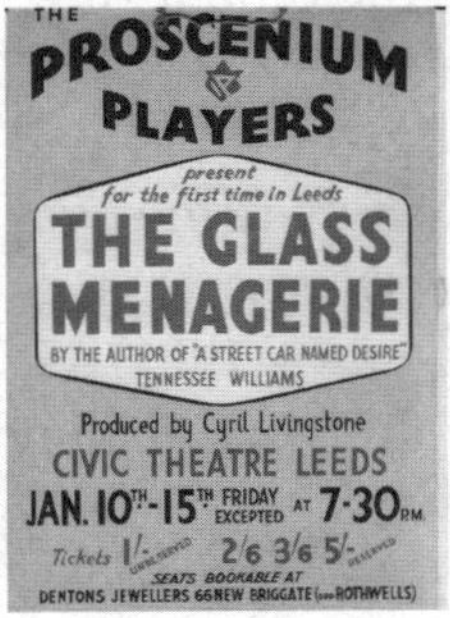

but also phoned his wife to tell her he would babysit on Saturday evening, so that she could attend a performance. It was a hold-the-front-page scenario and so exciting. I think Laura was one of the best performances I gave because I was acting against type and really lost myself in the interpretation. Cyril's direction throughout was finely tuned and nuanced. It was a delightful play.'

In March, 1955, Richard Courtney was invited to direct Pirandello's *Six Characters in Search of an Author*. In a new translation by Frederick May, it featured Philip Stone, an actor of extraordinary sensitivity and accomplishment who played The Father. Philip was a professional actor who was struck down with tuberculosis. He was forced to leave the profession, went into a sanatorium and underwent an operation during which the surgeon collapsed one of his lungs. He then went to live with an aunt in Grange-over-Sands, who made a room for him in an outhouse in the grounds of her home. Philip, however, made a remarkable recovery and returned to Leeds. With acting in his blood, he soon became attracted to the Leeds amateur stage movement and eventually met Alec Baron. Both men, steeped in theatre, became friends and would spend many happy hours 'talking shop' well into the night.

Leeds-born Philip Stones (he dropped the 's' when he entered the acting profession) came from a teaching family. His acting style was reminiscent of Ralph Richardson. With a resonant voice and restless, persuasive stage presence, he was expert at repose on stage and had a magnetic quality, even when standing still. Philip broke into theatre in London in 1947, acting in James Bridie's *The Sleeping Clergyman* at the Criterion. After his illness and his time recuperating in Leeds, he returned to the professional stage soon after leaving the Pross, starting with a stint in repertory. He then acted for Lindsay Anderson in David Storey's *The Contractor* (Royal Court 1969) where he was seen by film director Stanley Kubrick who cast him as Malcolm McDowell's 'Dad' in *A Clockwork Orange* (1971). He was also to feature in *Barry Lyndon* (1975) and *The Shining* (1980).

Philip appeared in two plays he admired enormously and of which he often referred during the many conversations I had with him when we shared the same dressing room at Leeds Civic Theatre. One was the Inspector in JB Priestley's *An Inspector Calls,* which he did for Bernard Miles in a much admired production at the Mermaid Theatre in 1973. The other was in 1979 as the Father in *Six Characters in Search of an Author,* where he repeated his eerily effective interpretation seen first with the Pross. Philip, who was to give me lots of advice about acting, ('less means more' being one of his many recommendations) died in London in June, 2003 aged 79.

The *Yorkshire Evening Post* thought the Pross production of *Six Characters in Search of an Author* a fine one. Apart from Philip's haunting portrayal, the newspaper singled out my own performance as the son, which amazed and delighted me because I had such a dreadful time in rehearsal. Courtney was not getting through to me and I knew that something about my performance was not quite right. So, I confided my frustration to Cyril after the last rehearsal. He very kindly agreed to attend the dress rehearsal and met me afterwards in the Civic Theatre corridor.

'You've got it all wrong,' he scolded. 'He's an angry young man, yes, but there are other ways of depicting anger without shouting. Play him in a lower key and keep his rage under control.'

So I took his advice and stayed up all night going through the part to make subtle changes that would not affect the other actors. When I turned up with my new toned-down characterisation everyone was amazed at the improvement and the following evening's *YEP* review confirmed my faith in the abilities of director Cyril Livingstone:

> John Fisher gave a thrilling performance as the Son and illustrated why the Proscenium Players have such high hopes for him; he is endowed with a stage presence quite out of keeping with his years.

The Way She Manhandles That Buick Makes Me Sick
The Big Knife

Clifford Odets's drama *The Big Knife* took the lid off Hollywood and followed the Pirandello into the Civic Theatre in April 1955. The play was directed by Cyril Livingstone, who also played the part of Hank Teagle. Odets became famous on Broadway for plays like *Waiting for Lefty* and *Golden Boy* and wrote taut, nervous dialogue. Hollywood was where Odets, once married to actress Claudette Colbert, worked for some considerable time.

The production introduced a dynamic actor called Jeffrey Smith, who played the role of Charles Castle. Jeffrey, who had directed a couple of Leeds University Rag Revues, scored a considerable success with this play and was later called in to direct future productions.

I suffered my first stage mishap just before the curtain rose on the first night.

As Buddy Bliss, a Hollywood PR man, I opened the play

Above: A scene from *Two On An Island* - Barry Cryer is seated reading, far right

with Jennie Stratton who played Patty Benedict, a Hedda Hopper type of gossip columnist. I was meant to be in an anxious state at our interview and had to enter and nervously light up a cigarette.

In rehearsal, Cyril kept giving me a note to act with more anxiety and even tremble a little when lighting the cigarette. To make me look older Cyril had requested I wear a moustache. Looking into the mirror just before I was called on stage I noticed that one side looked a little bedraggled so I asked fellow actor Cedric Vendyback, who played Smiley Coy, to quickly trim the hairs for me. He sat me down in a chair and started to clip away. Suddenly, I was aware of some liquid dripping on to my chin and saw Cedric turn white under his own make-up. 'I am so, so, so sorry,' he whispered - Smiley had snipped my lip and I wasn't laughing.

In those days the National Anthem was played before each performance and there we were asking God to save our Queen and there I was sitting in my dressing room haemorrhaging to death!

I was bleeding profusely and we just couldn't stem the flow of blood. After the anthem had finished we heard the clatter of seats go down and then that pregnant silence you get just before the start of a play. All I was saying under a mass of Kleenex toilet tissues was: 'I should be on stage, I should be on stage '.

Fortunately, Nevil Silverton who was in the flies supervising the lighting sensed something was wrong and came into the dressing room to see why I wasn't on stage. I don't know why he was carrying a styptic pencil in his overall but he was and miraculously whipped out this life-saver and, moistening it under the water tap, applied it to my lip. This eventually stopped the bleeding and I was ushered on to the stage a nervous wreck.

Of course no one out front was any the wiser but Marion Boyd our costumes supervisor did comment afterwards: 'You managed to get the anxiety in your first entrance alright, didn't you John?'

A few months prior to *The Big Knife* Alec was rummaging through a box of books outside a Leeds second-hand bookshop and came across a tattered copy of a little known play by Elmer Rice called *Two On An Island*. The piece was a love letter to New York, but what interested Alec was the fact that it was presented in cinematic format and almost a blueprint for a musical. He was intrigued by the diversity of the 11 sets required to tell the story of two naïve youngsters coming to the Big Apple to find fortune, romance and eventually love. The settings included Broadway, the subway (in motion), Greenwich Village, a diner, a tour bus, the Metropolitan Museum of Modern Art and the top of the Statue of Liberty. It had a cast of 40 and presented Alec with a challenge to use the resources of the Civic Theatre to the full. It was also a British premiere.

Alec gathered all the talent that the group possessed. The young lovers, bursting with love and ambition, were played by Mavis Addleman and me. The couple appear in every scene in the play but do not actually meet until the very end, pre-empting Nora Ephron's 1996 film *Sleepless in Seattle*. Comedian Barry Cryer, playing a lovely cameo role as a sightseeing guide, was duly noticed and praised by the local press, and Cyril Livingstone was splendid as Lawrence Ormont, the cynical Broadway producer. The production, presented week commencing Monday, October 17, 1955, stretched the talents of the group to the limit and was greatly admired, but the critics found holes in the play which they thought was too thin and lacking in focus.

About this time, the group had launched a new venture which they named The Sunday Club. This was presented in a room at the Griffin Hotel on Boar Lane every two weeks. A charge of 2/- (two shillings) was made to members and visitors were asked to pay an extra membership fee of 6d (six pennies). Prominent local producers, critics, theatre people and writers were all invited to be guest speakers, and none ever refused. For example Vivian Daniels, a renowned director of BBC Drama for the North region, spoke on producing radio drama, and Richard Courtney, who was also the editor of a magazine called *Act*, gave a short lecture on running a theatrical magazine. Philip Stone and his fiancée Margaret Pickard presented a charming programme of poems, prose and verse. There was also a workshop production of Christopher Fry's *A Phoenix Too Frequent*, with an extra charge to the audience of one shilling per head that went towards paying for the royalties.

The group also held *Any Theatre Questions*, a panel game with question and answer sessions, as well as short theatrical pieces and play excerpts. At any given Sunday evening a visitor could expect to see excerpts from *Under Milk Wood, The Cherry Orchard* or *Hamlet*. The club fulfilled a need not only for the group's own members but also for many non-members, who were interested in theatre. The

Above: Frederick Spencer and John Fisher in *The Duke In Darkness*, 1955

Sunday Club became the 'in place' to go and attracted a cult following.

One of the Club's greatest successes, however, was a fine, moving production of Pirandello's *The Man With a Flower in His Mouth*, directed by Alec Baron and starring Philip Stone. The Sunday Club was also strong on debate and one Sunday in March held a discussion with Leeds Art Theatre. The Motion was that: 'This House is of the opinion that the Amateur Groups at the Civic Theatre get the audiences they deserve.' The Chairman for the evening was Philip Wright, a distinguished member of Leeds Art Theatre and the ambivalence of the Motion turned out some interesting and hilarious observations.

Other illustrious celebrities to attend the Sunday Club meetings were Patrick Campbell from the British Drama League and the BBC, Lawrence Storm, resident producer of Harry Hanson's Court Players and the legendary Rudi

Shelly from the Bristol Old Vic Theatre School (BOVTS). Shelly's appearance at the Sunday Club was quite a scoop and attracted a record crowd. He had joined the BOVTS teaching staff two weeks after the school opened in 1946 and was still working well into his nineties. Over the years many established actors from around the world sought out Shelly's masterclasses when visiting or working in England. Cyril Livingstone recalled various drama groups presenting a programme of critiques.

'A few of us became theatre critics and we reviewed the Leeds Civic Theatre drama season. I remember giving a scathing review to Leeds Art Theatre's *A Month in the Country* which starred Peter O'Toole and was interminable. I said: "More like a year in the theatre than a month in the country." O'Toole never spoke to me again.'

However, Leeds Art Theatre got their own back when reviewing the Pross' production of *The Miser* by saying: 'Cyril Livingstone's production of Moliere's *The Miser* was so full of charm you could have sliced it with a knife'.

A White Horse!
The Duke In Darkness

The Pross was now giving other members the opportunity to direct. Cedric Vendyback had played quite a few character parts with the company and had scored quite heavily with his interpretation of Tom Wingfield, the son in *The Glass Menagerie.* For the winter production 1955, he chose Patrick Hamilton's *The Duke in Darkness* a play with an all-male cast.

The piece was written in the late 1930s and was set in 16th century France. Its theme was freedom from oppression and had a very modern message. The Duke of Laterraine had been imprisoned for 15 years but, for five years, had feigned blindness whilst plotting his escape. It was an immense part and Frederick Spencer played it to the hilt. Frederick was from the old school and although not exactly hanging from the curtains for his bows, was a stickler for diction and enunciation. He had an important scene with Cyril Livingstone - who played the wicked Duke of Lamorre

- in which there was a line that ended with '...a white horse?' Frederick insisted that the word be pronounced 'wphewite'. Cyril, on the other hand, insisted the word be spoken as 'wite.' Neither would surrender and the scene became something of a ping-pong match with no player really winning.

This historical thriller received a good press, particularly from Angus Turner, writing in the *YEP*. 'There was an excitement from start to finish,' he wrote and continued to praise the acting and particularly the magnificent set, which was designed professionally by Paul Bernard, who designed mostly for television.

After the success of Philip Stone's brilliant performance in *The Man with a Flower in His Mouth* at the Sunday Club, Alec persuaded Philip to repeat this performance at the Leeds Civic Theatre. After major surgery Philip had become wary of doing any more acting because of his breathing problems and particularly for a whole week. So determined was he, though, to play this role that he underwent a strict routine of physiotherapy and regular breathing exercises and managed to get himself fit and psychologically right. Alec would incorporate this one-act play into the Proscenium's next production called *Spotlight*, a compilation of three short plays. The Pirandello shared the bill with Christopher Fry's *A Phoenix Too Frequent* (directed by Cyril Livingstone) and J.M. Barrie's delightful *Shall We Join the Ladies*, which Alec directed week commencing April 20, 1953.

The Barrie was one of my favourite pieces. It was set in the dining room of Sam Smith's country house and was very reminiscent of an Agatha Christie drama, where suspicion falls on every character in the play. Cyril played Sam Smith and reminded everyone of Dickens's Mr. Pickwick. Alec directed the play with impeccable taste. Thirteen people were seated around an elegant dining table which had been

Above: Was *The Miser* full of charm? Leeds Art Theatre appeared to think so...

beautifully set out with sparkling glassware, silver cutlery and a choice dinner service. All the characters looked amazing; the ladies in long evening gowns and the men in dress suits. Its opening line, 'We are 13 at table!' amused us all and was brought out at every dinner party thereafter.

Alec's friend Frederick May, a professor of the Italian department at Leeds University and a man of the theatre, had also contracted tuberculosis. During his time in Killingbeck hospital he had been working on a new translation of *The Man with a Flower in His Mouth*. Alec was keen to present May's version and dates were fixed for him to receive the completed manuscript. Unfortunately Frederick took a turn for the worse and the translation was not ready by the time rehearsals began, so Alec used another version. The translation was received, however, two weeks before the play's opening and passed on to Philip for his perusal. The play opened in the week commencing February 13, 1956 and received a rave reaction from both audience and critics. Reading of the success of the play in the press

Frederick, still in hospital but making a remarkable recovery, asked permission to be escorted by a nurse to see the last performance and witness his translation being performed. He informed Alec of his decision on the morning after the show opened. In a great panic and with huge embarrassment Alec phoned Philip and informed him that he just had to learn Frederick's translation in time for the Saturday night performance. Philip came up trumps and gave another triumphant performance. This was to be the only performance Philip gave of Frederick's translation and May was delighted with the result, little knowing the agitation his visit had caused.

In April 1956, the Players turned to a classic for their spring production. Cyril Livingstone directed a stylish version of Oscar Wilde's *A Woman of No Importance*. The play had recently received a lavish and fresh professional production in the West End and Cyril was attracted to the absence of melodrama in the new adaptation.

The play received favourable reviews, with Desmond Pratt of the *Yorkshire Post* commenting that the production must surely be the city's most sumptuous amateur production of the year. 'The two scenes are miracles of period furnishing and decoration,' he wrote.

The play, Wilde's second-largest stage success, was rarely performed mainly because of its over-the-top content. 'Stop! Gerald, stop. He is your father!' - to quote but one show-stopper. The theme of the play is that of a woman betrayed and scorned by society, but Paul Dehn had written a more up-to-date version, clearing away the dead wood. Philip Stone gave a lovely self-assured performance as Lord Illingworth and Jane Platt brought sincerity and grace to Mrs. Arbuthnot, the 'woman' of the title.

The Players had always wanted to produce a musical. For many years the idea of presenting *The Threepenny Opera* had been bandied about, but this was quickly discarded. As a compromise and for the opening production of the new season in October 1956, they 'timidly' presented a crazy, mixed-up revue called *Sweet and Sour*. This was to prove more difficult to produce than a full-length play, but to their credit the group did a magnificent job. Alec directed and the choreography was by Joyce Adcock, who together with Gordon Caleb contributed some very witty ditties. Rosalyn Whyman confirmed that she had a real talent for quick fire revue and her Eartha Kitt impersonation in 'Monotonous' was a delight. Jeffrey Smith wrote a cracking number called 'Scandal at the Handels', a cleverly observed piece about young George Frederic driving his neighbours round the bend with his late night composing.

Sue Appleson, who was then a young Susan Lewis who had been trained in dancing, also appeared in the show. 'It was very exciting indeed because it was my first production and I had only just joined the group. I wasn't expecting to be in the show because it had already been cast. However, unfortunately for one girl, but fortunately for me, she had to drop out due to illness. I was given the opportunity to appear in the revue and had a wonderful week singing and dancing in the chorus. It was also quite an achievement for the rest of the group because they had all been accustomed to appear only in drama, so to suddenly add singing and dancing to their repertoire was a triumph. They were all terrific.'

In January 1957, the group presented George Bellak's tense drama *The Troublemakers,* set in an American University town. It told the tragedy of a family who lose their son in a killing at the university and the torment of a student who witnesses the death and who is forced into action when he senses the perpetrators are likely to get away with their crime.

The play, directed by Jeffrey Smith, produced a most realistic fight scene and had an interesting split-level set, alternating between the university and the family home. In its 11 scenes it produced some inventive lighting by Alec. Jenny Stratton, as the boy's mother, and Philip Stone, as the tutor, excelled in the acting department.

I was now 20 years old and originally cast as Torin, the victim. But because of casting difficulties when the original actor dropped out during rehearsals, I finished up playing the boy's father!

The Prima Donna And The Herring

One day Alec phoned me to say a famous New York Yiddish theatre actress called Cecelia Lipson was in Leeds to stage a play at the Jubilee Hall and had approached him to find someone to play the role of her son.

'She is doing a play written by herself called *The Kuni-Lemil*. I think you would make a good job of the son and it would give you some experience acting with a professional actress,' he advised. So, I said yes.

Miss Lipson was lodging in a house in Mexborough Avenue and after telephoning her I made an appointment for the two of us to meet. Armed with a copy of Stanislavsky's *An Actor Prepares,* I turned up on Miss Lipson's doorstep.

I rang the doorbell and a woman in her seventies, dressed in a voluminous chiffon house-coat greeted me. She sported enormous pink bunny-rabbit slippers and a lighted cigarette dangled from the corner of an over-painted mouth. She was very theatrical.

I was shown into the front parlour, which housed a single bed on which rested three suitcases. Two were thrown open with clothes scattered all over the place. In the corner of the room there was a small table with a chunk of black bread and a half-eaten pickled herring on a plate.

'So you're from the Proscenium Players,' she said with a New York drawl that stretched from Chapeltown Road to Moortown Corner. 'What kind of plays do they perform,' she asked, but didn't wait for me to reply.

The actress informed me that she had decided not to stage *The Kuni-Lemil* but to perform *A Mother's Grief* instead.

'You are to play Yossel, my soldier son returning to a mother who's been left alone, neglected, starved and desolate in a Brooklyn tenement and now dying of tuberculosis. Do you think you can manage that?' she asked waving the cigarette in my face.

'Er, yes, of course,' I coughed through the smoke. 'May I see the script?'

'Script?' she spluttered. 'Who needs a script? Bernard Shaw does scripts - my words come from the heart.'

'But how will I know my cues?' I asked breathlessly.

'You'll sense them, darling,' she replied.

My gaze fell on the pickled herring - I am sure it moved.

The first scene started with the diva seated centre stage and crying, her body swaying to and fro, her arms reaching up to the heavens above. Yiddish actors did an awful lot of crying, I thought. 'Ratevet fun hunger mikh astind (Save me from hunger now),' she cried and immediately reached out for a fork to spike a piece of herring.

I had been given a few lines to say at different intervals. I soon got the gist of it, whenever there was a pause and Miss Lipson looked sideways that was my cue to jump in.

My first entrance started with a stunner. 'Mamma, mamma, it's me, Yossel.'

'No!' she screamed at me. 'Don't give me Shakespeare! I want Garfield in *Awake and Sing* not Gielgud in *King Lear.*' She sat back in her chair and continued crying and rocking back and forth. She terrified me half to death.

'Go away now, darling. I'm exhausted. See you tomorrow, same time, same place, and no more Shakespeare, please!'

I returned the next day with a perfected Brooklyn accent to be greeted with: 'I've changed the piece, darling. I'm not doing *Shmendrik of the Bronx.* '

'But we're rehearsing *A Mother's Grief,*' I corrected.

Ignoring me, she spiked another piece of herring.

The star said she'd like to give the people of Leeds *Dos Pintele Yid* or even *Di Shtume Kale*. But she didn't think they were ready for those masterpieces, so instead they 'were gonna get *Fun Zayn Fidl Der Klang,*' a title roughly translated, I think, as 'The Sounds from his Fiddle', which didn't quite fit Miss Lipson's scenario of deprivation and suffering.

'You play my son, Mendele, and he's a sailor,' she said. She certainly liked the military, I thought.

'What do I say?' I nervously enquired.

'Same lines as before, darling, and remember give me Garfield.'

The atmosphere of the room suddenly became stifling and I wondered how many play-titles we would go through before she eventually decided on the final play.

Maybe I should have persevered, but I found myself apologising and telling her I had second thoughts and felt it necessary to decline the offer to appear in her lovely play(s). 'OK, if that's what you want,' she said dismissively. 'Just one thing, darling. Would you go to the shop on the next block and buy me a black-bread and a pickled herring?'

I ran down the path, rushed into the delicatessen and ran all the way back to her front door. I flung the food into her hands along with the change from a ten shilling note. On the journey homewards I opened *An Actor Prepares* and consulted Stanislavsky for guidance.

'The organic bases of the laws of nature on which our art is formed will protect you in the future from going down the wrong path,' he clearly stated. Pushing Stanislavsky to the bottom of my brief case I pulled out a copy of the Pross' next production and proceeded home to sanity and a strong cup of tea.

Cecelia Lipson was born in New York on September 15, 1892 and died in New York on November 5, 1979.

In 1969, she was featured in John Schlesinger's film *Midnight Cowboy*. She played an eccentric theatrical in the psychedelic party sequence. Seated on a sofa surrounded by admirers and dressed in white satin, bedecked with jewels she said: 'I love everything in the theatre. I would love to die on the stage.'

Sip On The Crater Is The First
First Confession Of The Chilled Pumpkin
Pantagleize

Jeffrey Smith was again called upon to direct the April 1957 production of Giraudoux's *The Mad Woman of Chaillot*. The play's philosophy, that money was the root of all evil, delighted audiences throughout the week.

Angus Turner noted in the *YEP* that it was one of the outstanding productions of the season and singled out, from a cast of 40, John Linstrum's superb performance as the Rag Picker, played by Danny Kaye on Broadway, and Jane Platt's playing of Countess Aurelia, cleverly alternating between her fantasy world and the dangers surrounding her in real life. I played the Prospector and I remember Cyril giving me a few tips on how to play him, one being an American drawl which was highly reminiscent of the Yiddish actress I nearly played opposite.

The play was to be adapted in 1969 by Jerry Herman as a Broadway musical called *Dear World*. Despite the casting of wonderful Angela Lansbury it ran for only 162 performances.

It was in October 1957 that the Players had the opportunity to present a serious work, and a World premiere at that. Alec Baron had a friend called George Hauger who was Lecturer of Drama at the Extra-Mural department at Leeds University. George was a great admirer of the Proscenium Players and a frequent speaker at the Sunday Club. He was also the English translator of the Belgian dramatist Michel de Ghelderode. George had just completed the translation of de Ghelderode's massive and probably greatest work, *Pantagleize*.

He asked if Alec would be interested in directing this world premiere. In fact, it was to be the first production of any de Ghelderode play translated into English. Alec loved the play and, with a few alterations, decided to stage it in Leeds. It had a cast of 23 speaking parts, mostly men, and it required a Chaplinesque comedian in the leading role. Alec had recently spotted an excellent actor called Kenneth Paine, who acted with the Bingley Players, and who jumped at the offer to play this theatrical eccentric.

The play was set in Europe on the morrow of one war and the eve of another and followed Pantagleize on the day of his 40th birthday.

Pantagleize writes for a fashion magazine and he has been told that on this day his destiny will begin and decides to greet everyone with the phrase 'What a lovely day!', unaware that this is the signal for the planned uprising of the Liberals to begin. He is observed by a plain-clothes policeman, and a group of revolutionaries who are gathered in a cafe where our hero goes to take morning coffee. Greeting everyone with the phrase, he sparks off the revolution and is hailed as their leader.

Pantagleize was billed as a farce to make you sad, and attracted critics from some of the national newspapers to attend its first night.

Above: John Fisher is Roderigo and Philip Stone Cassio in *Othello*, 1957

Because of the technicalities of lighting, sound, quick scenery changes, the dress rehearsal over-ran four hours, and the company did not leave the theatre till well after 2am, prompting one performer to murmur: 'Who do I have to sleep with to get out of here?'

As most of the cast had to get up for work the next morning, there were lots of bleary-eyed actors passing through the stage door on opening night. However, the play's the thing and we all managed to rise to the occasion

Cedric Gould played Bamboola and had to be blacked up for the part. Stanley Sher excelled as the revolutionary waiter and I was cast as the poet Blank and had a whale of a time camping it up, especially in the trial scene where I had to justify my poetry with a two-minute example of my work which was recited without a pause and was a jumble of nonsensical words: 'Sip on the crater is the first first confession of the chilled pumpkin losing all its stuffed marrow the lovely child sucking the mauve star the Arab had melted the worm lonely and blue ...', which I still use as a warming up exercise whenever I do any public speaking.

Towards the end of the play most of the revolutionaries are killed, and that included me. We had to `play dead` on stage for at least five minutes, which is a long time when you are longing to scratch your nose. 'John, I can still see you breathing!' shouted Alec from the stalls at the dress rehearsal.

The first night was presented before an invited charity audience fundraising for the Multiple Sclerosis Society who clearly felt bewildered by the play's political message, but subsequent audiences during the two-week run reacted to the play enthusiastically, as did the critics. However, most felt that the play was far, far too long.

The *Manchester Guardian* stated that the production was most adroitly presented, stylised and balletic, with worthy sets and costumes. Their critic also heaped praise on Kenneth Paine's performance. The *Yorkshire Post* commented that the colour of the production, the crowd scenes, simple evocative settings and lighting were a constant delight as was the acting.

Many years later, Alec and his wife Judith were holidaying in Ostend and discovered a permanent de Ghelderode exhibition in the James Ensor House. Inside were stills from the Leeds production, press reviews, a published script with the original Leeds cast, as well as a long letter that the author had sent to Leeds apologising for his absence on the first night because of illness. The dramatist was to die shortly after the Leeds production.

On December 8, 1957, Cyril Livingstone staged a banned play at Bradford Civic Playhouse's Theatre Club. This was to prove to be the most controversial staging of any play the group was to present and provoked a slew of letters to the editor in two of Bradford's newspapers, culminating in a long, strong defence by George Hauger of the play's merits and Jean-Paul Sartre's virtues.

Sartre's *Huis Clos* (In Camera) had been banned from being staged in England by the Lord Chamberlain.

However, it was allowed to be seen privately and the Theatre Club and its members came under this jurisdiction. Sartre was France's leading pessimist in the philosophy of existentialism. 'When you die, you're dead,' one character says to another, and the play dealt with three people being locked in a room together for eternity and coined the famous phrase 'Hell is other People.'

Appearing in the play were Peter Cariss, Thelma Rose, Zelda Statman and myself as the menacing Valet, a part originally played in London by Donald Pleasance and one which I relished. After the performance, George Hauger gave a talk entitled *Signposts to Sartre* which spotlighted the basic principles of the author's philosophy.

The morning after the play was performed, Cyril Livingstone received phone calls from the executive committee at Bradford Civic saying that the play had created a storm of protest. Many letters had been sent to the Bradford newspapers by people concerned about the content of the play, which many found offensive and accused the organisers of 'dirty minded preoccupation.'

George Hauger suddenly found himself as a contentious figure in the Bradford press and felt compelled to defend his comments in print when replying to a Shipley reader's barbarous observations on Hauger's lecture.

'Lecturer Defends the Giving of Sartre Play' was the headline of an article in Bradford's *Telegraph and Argus*. Mr. Hauger had asked to be allowed to correct the impression that he had been acting as 'master of ceremonies in a house of ill-fame'. This referred to a comment in a letter by an irate reader who described the evening as 'deeply offensive and nauseating'. He or she simply signed the letter, Shipley Reader. Hauger counter-attacked: 'The only person really privileged to condemn a play as offensive is he who can demonstrate the play's offensiveness by quoting chapter and

Above: Alan Marshall. Cedric Gould, John Fisher, Jennie Stratton in *Doctor Knock*

verse. Your "Shipley Reader" does not do that for *Huis Clos*.' Hauger then cited the reader's observations of the play's theme of sexual perversion and Sartre's passion for cruelty and female homosexuality and commented: 'Surely these are subjects about whom we, and especially last night's audience, would like to know more.' The reader retaliated: 'Mr. Hauger takes me to task for condemning *Huis Clos* as offensive. This I did not do. I made no criticism of the play at all. I merely commented on its characters, a sadist, a lesbian and a child murderer - a pretty offensive sounding trio.'

The correspondent then added that Bradford Civic Theatre Club appeared always to choose plays with unpleasant characters and themes, signing off with the telling comment: 'Wasn't the previous Theatre Club production a play about rape?'

For their next production in December 1957 Jeffrey Smith was again invited to direct. This time he turned to Shakespeare and chose *The Tragedy of Othello.* The Players had discovered a black actor called James Allen Jones, who

Above: John Fisher, Thelma Rose, Cyril Livingstone and Sadie Crown in *The Waltz of the Toreadors* in 1959

was cast as the noble Moor. James was an American teacher working in Leeds on an exchange teacher scheme and was very charming and affable, but audiences felt, although it was an interesting experiment, his strong American accent and style of acting were unconvincing.

Desmond Pratt writing in the *Yorkshire Post* thought that the frightening sense of jealousy and passion were sadly lacking in James' performance. He praised Smith's excellent staging and liked Anthony Haigh's sinister Iago, Pat Wurzal as a tender Desdemona, the well-spoken Emilia from Sadie Cornick and John Fisher's foppish Roderigo, 'flitting like a useless moth around the candle of intrigue.' But he felt the Othello was wrong and concluded that this was a Moor without romance, and surely this was one of literature's great romantic figures.

Do You Smoke? Stop it! Do You Drink? Drop it! Are You Married? Forget it! *Doctor Knock*

Jeffrey Smith was, however, to be given another chance and for the February 1958 production chose Jules Romain's satire of the medical profession *Doctor Knock*, in a translation by Harley Granville Barker.

The setting of the first act focused around a motor car, circa 1900, and Alf Rowley, a specialist in shop display, was asked to design and build a life-size model of a 1902 Panhard. This venture took Alf two months and the result was a surefire hit, as was the play. It was a slightly dated piece about a young doctor who arrives in a sleepy French town where no one is ever ill. Together with the local pharmacist he conspires to alter the situation and by the final curtain the villagers are all hypochondriacs and the doctor's practice changed beyond all recognition.

In this production I was given my first leading part as Dr. Knock. *YEP* critic Angus Turner commented that it was a triumph. 'The production stands or falls by the performance of Dr. Knock,' he wrote, 'and the society has made an excellent choice in John Fisher. He is an outstanding young actor who seems to revel in parts much senior to his actual years.' The *Yorkshire Post* thought the production had vitality and sparkle and was 'a cure for many ills'. It gave the group the chance to present some fine cameo playing, and Jennie Stratton, Val Gallagher and Renee Hipshon turned in some 'top-quality acting'.

1958 was the centenary year of the Leeds Triennial Musical Festival and to mark this cultural event the Proscenium Players was asked to provide a late night entertainment at the Leeds City Varieties. Following on from the success of their revue *Sweet and Sour*, the committee decided upon another revue. The Varieties staged a special all-star bill, which included Randolph Sutton, Jimmy Wheeler, Leslie Randall, Gladys Morgan, Elizabeth Larner and Leeds revue star Thelma Ruby. It was presented at 6.15pm and 8.15pm and the Proscenium revue went on at 10.30pm until midnight.

The show, called *On the Verge*, was to be the first intimate late night revue to be played in Leeds and was staged without an interval. Collaborators Joyce Adcock and Gordon Caleb, who later went professional, wrote all the music and lyrics for the show. One of the highlights was an amusing number entitled 'We're All that's Left of the YSO', presented by a five-piece Palm Court orchestra who were all that was left of the sadly defunct Yorkshire Symphony Orchestra. The star of the show was undoubtedly Rosalyn Whyman, who made quite a name for herself in the show's major sketches, particularly scoring as Eartha Kitt in a rendition of 'Monotonous'. Jeffrey Smith's brilliant 'Scandal at the Handel's' was again used to stunning effect and the number was televised in Manchester by BBC TV on their round up of the Festival news, entitled *Looking North*.

The Pross also scored another 'first,' this time on BBC Radio Leeds. Extensive modernisation had been carried out at the BBC studios in Woodhouse Lane. These were the first major modernisations executed since the Leeds studios opened in 1932. The first sound broadcast direct from Studio One took place on October 14, when the Pross was invited to present excerpts from *On the Verge*.

The show became the talk of the town, with queues for tickets around the theatre every night. The opera company who were presenting Handel's *Samson and Delilah* at Leeds Grand Theatre had heard about the show and sent for 100 tickets for any performance, but as the show was a complete sell-out the box office sadly had to decline the booking.

Still in the mood for comedy, the Players then presented Anouilh's *The Waltz of the Toreadors,* in the week commencing January 26, 1959. Cedric Vendyback was the director and the charming, stylised sets were designed by Leslie Wainwright. This was a farce that piled absurdity upon absurdity with bitter undertones of loneliness.

Cedric, however, did not quite manage to strike a satisfying balance between tragedy and comedy and wasn't quite sure whether to play for laughs or concentrate on the poignant aspects of the piece. Consequently the key scene in Act Three between the General and his wife seemed incompatible.

Cyril Livingstone played the lonely General St. Pe, and Desmond Pratt writing in the *Yorkshire Post* thought that he sustained the long and arduous role with great skill. His bed-ridden Valkyrie of a wife was played with force by Sadie Crown.

Above: Rosalyn Whyman and John Fisher as Mr. and Mrs. Pugh, *Under Milk Wood*

Someone Now Knows We're Up Here
The Diary Of Anne Frank

Anne Frank, born in 1929 in Frankfurt am Main, Germany, is now widely known throughout the world. She stands as a symbol of millions of people who suffered and perished just like her. Anne's famous diary, however, is not by any means the morbid chronicle that so many visualise and, in 1955/56, it was adapted by Frances Goodrich and Albert Hackett for the Broadway stage where it received critical acclaim and won all the top prizes.

In 1958, it opened in the West End. Soon the Proscenium Players were hot on its trail for the amateur rights. After much pressure and soft talking the society was duly given permission to present the play, *The Diary of Anne Frank,* for the first time in Leeds. On week commencing April 13, 1959, it opened to packed houses, directed by Cyril Livingstone, who invested a great deal of detail in set and characterisations and provided the cast with the right amount of research into the Anne Frank story.

Rehearsals had been strained at first. There were

problems getting the 'right Anne' and the group went through two or three potentials before settling on local actress Pat Wurzal, who eventually turned in a spirited and sensitive performance. The play also introduced newcomer Michael Kent as Otto Frank. Michael was an experienced actor/director who hailed from London, where he had worked with various amateur dramatic groups. He gave a movingly profound performance. Martin Glynne played young Peter, while Joe Stephenson and Rosalyn Whyman took the roles of Mr. and Mrs. Van Daan. I played Mr. Dussel the dentist, a role that I was to reprise many years later for Limelight Drama Group, whose production was one of the first to be seen at Leeds newest theatre, The Carriageworks.

Demand for tickets was phenomenal as nearly all of the Jewish community wanted to see the play. We had queues right down the steps of Leeds Civic Theatre waiting for returns. After a fantastic week the group decided to reprise the production a few weeks later where again it became the hottest ticket in town. It won the Leeds Civic Arts Guild awards for Best Production and Best Actor trophy for Michael Kent.

In November 1959, the group decided to stage Donald Ogden Stewart's *The Kidders*. It was directed by Cedric Vendyback and had a stylish living room set designed by Leslie Wainwright. The play had been a mild success in London but never quite came up to expectations. It had a cast of seven headed by Michael Kent, Pauline Bedford and Bill Tordoff.

Donald Ogden Stewart was born in Columbus, Ohio in 1894 and served in the US Navy during World War One. He was to become a screenwriter who specialised in adapting for the screen the work of others. He was the most prominent of such screenwriters and a supreme play doctor of the 1930s and '40s, plus an expert in tightening up loose ends. His career rested on seven films, the best of these being *Holiday* and *The Philadelphia Story*, for which he won an Academy Award.

Not unusually for the Communist-fearing times, Stewart's political involvement with the Hollywood Anti-Nazi League resulted in his studio, MGM, demanding he answer questions before the House on Un-American Activities Committee (HUAC), which he refused to do and was therefore blacklisted. With the help of Ruth Gordon and Garson Kanin he tried out *The Kidders* in Massachusetts in 1951 but found no Broadway takers, so the following year he brought the play to London. He died in London in August 1980.

It was around this time that I was invited to be in a Leeds University Rag Revue. Directed by Barrington Black, a 26-year-old Leeds solicitor and former President of Leeds University Union, Barry was for two years Vice-President of the National Union of Students, for whom he travelled widely as a representative in such countries as Russia, Hungary, Rumania and Czechoslovakia.

The show was staged at Leeds Empire and it was the thirtieth rag revue to be held in the city. Rag itself began in Leeds in the early 1920's and *Rag Ragout* emerged some years later at the Little Theatre in Leeds. It was an immediate success and was followed by others, produced in alternate years. Then as the organisation of the Student's Rag Week grew their Rag Revue became an annual show, attracted larger audiences and finally migrated to the Empire Theatre. The original book for the 1959 Revue was compiled from material by movers and shakers Michael Lamming, Leslie

Farrar, Joyce Adcock and Gordon Caleb. Choreography was by Cynthia Carr and the musical director was Terry Shaw.

This was a really happy show and I enjoyed myself enormously. Barry gave me some really good sketches to do, particularly a number called Peter Patter with Diane Hotchkins, a lovely leggy beauty with a husky voice who, as Diane Gaunt, appeared in a few Proscenium Players shows in the late 1960's. I also did an angry young man sketch about playwright John Osborne whose plays were all the rage; I joined the cast in a hilarious number sending-up a company from the Ukraine who had been touring the UK. It was called 'The Urinals Ensemble' and as Mikhail Fisherofskervitch I got to sing in faux-Russian which was then translated into English by a British announcer with an affected BBC accent. Acting on the Leeds Empire stage was like living the dream; it was a beautiful old theatre and had an enchantment all of its own.

The *Yorkshire Evening Post* critic raved about the show but, as luck would have it, there was a newspaper strike the day after the first night and the piece was never printed. Martin Glynne managed to get hold of the critique and posted it outside the theatre.

Entering the swinging sixties was an exciting time. The Pross decided to get things going with a piece that had long been on its list, Dylan Thomas's radio play, *Under Milk Wood*. Thomas introduced us to a fascinating view of life in a mythical Welsh village. The characters are almost cartooned but what is seen and heard of them is part of their essential reality. Hidden thoughts that would embarrass the conventional world are spoken aloud; real and conventional lives are in continual conflict once we are aware of them. Cyril Livingstone's production was ablaze with action and he brought a village to life with the resources available at Leeds Civic Theatre. He even built out into the orchestra pit and presented an imaginative seascape with the sound of running water, fishing nets and actors 'swimming' beneath.

Written for radio, *Under Milk Wood* was actually a 'play for voices', crowded with sparkling cameos. Cyril managed to bring out the irregularity and eccentricity of human behaviour in some inspired characterisations. David Hurst was in fine voice playing the Narrator and Bill Tordoff turned in a clever study of Captain Cat. Myrtle Young made a rather sedate and strict Mrs Ogmore-Pritchard and June Moss was a suitably pert Lily Smalls.

June was to marry solicitor Peter Fingret some years later and recalls: 'I was a rather shy 20-something when I was cast as Lily. I was absolutely in awe of the Pross acting talent and I loved every minute of the play, except perhaps the moment when Cyril, in his capacity as a director, shouted at me because I was too shy to lift my dress up and tuck it into my knickers when I scrubbed Butcher Beynon's door-steps. So, Cyril tucked it in for me and, boy oh boy, was I glad I was wearing big, thick navy blue under pants! I was teaching at the time and a group of my primary school children joined the cast. I was bursting with pride, they were so disciplined and eager to learn. Lily Smalls was the nicest part I ever had to play and I still remember it today with great joy, as well as the amazing production which was highly professional and simply wonderful to appear in.'

Rosalyn Whyman and I played Mr. and Mrs. Pugh and provided the biggest laughs of the evening, much to our amazement; our characterisations eventually being rewarded with Best Supporting Performance trophies at the Leeds Civic Arts Guild Awards later in the year. The production was also voted the Best Production of the Year. Desmond Pratt congratulated the cast of nearly 60 for having risen admirably to their immense task. 'The production had a precision of speech; at times almost verging on choric prose and a continual suggestion of the Welsh voice,' he said.

The week after *Under Milk Wood* was staged I received a charming letter from TV and stage director David Giles. David was the son of a dentist and educated at Shipley Grammar School. Due to be called up in the final months of the Second World War he was directed into the mines as a Bevin Boy but transferred later to the Royal Army Education Corps. David was to go on and direct some early *The Forsyte Saga* episodes for BBC in 1967, as well as *The Barchester Chronicles* in 1982. An innovative director, he worked with The Actors' Company formed by Sir Ian McKellen. For the West Yorkshire Playhouse he directed *Smoking With Lulu*, which later transferred to London.

David had seen *Milk Wood* and enjoyed my 'deliciously snide performance as Mr Pugh'. He invited me to play the Beadle (to Pontius Pilate) in the 1960 York Festival Society's production of *The York Cycle of Mystery Plays*, which I accepted. Also invited to appear in the production were Cyril Livingstone, who was cast as Caiaphas, and Valentine Gallagher and Michael Brennan, who had also been in *Milk Wood*. Our travelling companion was a professional actor from Leeds called Clifford Parrish, who played the part of the Prophet in the second scene.

The five of us travelled by train from Leeds to York and then a taxi was laid on to bring us all back to Leeds after the show. Our talk was mostly theatrical and I just loved listening to Clifford regale amusing anecdotes about people he had worked with in the profession.

Appearing in the *Mystery Plays* was a fine experience for me. They were performed in the gardens of St Mary's Abbey, hailed in the Middle Ages as the greatest abbey in the North of England. The plays were staged from June 12 to July 3, 1960, commencing in daylight and finishing under floodlight.

Above: Myrtle Young and John Fisher in *Hotel Paradiso*, February 1961

The Beadle was a really showy cameo and David and I milked it for all it was worth. He made my character appear to be Pilate's 'bit-on-the-side', which certainly gave a new meaning to The Sermon on the Mount.

Cyril, Val, Michael and I spent a delightful afternoon with David Giles and set-designer Kenneth Mellor in their rented accommodation in York, when afternoon tea was laid on for us. I also recall striking up a nice friendship with a woman who was in the costumes department and also played a peasant in the crowd scenes. Her name was Olave Dench, a *Mystery Plays* stalwart. Her daughter Judi, an actress, had played the part of Mary in the 1957 *Mystery Plays* (in which David Giles appeared) and was making quite a name for herself at the Old Vic in London. Judi, who was educated at York's Mount School, came to see the dress rehearsal and Olave told me afterwards that she asked her mother who was the boy 'with the strong, clear voice'.

Above: Frank Cox, Thelma Rose, Vivienne Jacobs, John Fisher and Ronald Pickup get to grips with Dostoevsky's *Crime and Punishment* in 1962

'That's John Fisher; he's from the Proscenium Players, you know,' Olave said in her Irish lilt. 'He's quite good,' Judi replied.

We were honoured to have the Queen Mother attend one of the performances and she came backstage to see the company afterwards. Cyril, along with other leading actors, was introduced to her and then Her Majesty wandered over to my little crowd and commented that she was surprised to see so many young people in the company. Were we all students, she enquired? Also in the cast was a wonderful professional actor called Harold Lang who, as Lucifer, slid down a huge flight of stairs like a serpent for his first entrance. Veteran actor Robert Eddison played God, on-stage and off. He had his own caravan to rest in and hardly mingled with the rest of the company. He also had a magnificent stage presence and a voice to melt steel. David Giles, who was born in October, 1926 died in January 2010.

Following the enormous success of *Under Milk Wood,* Cyril came up with a play that had probably evoked more controversy and criticism on morality grounds than any other post war drama. Tennessee Williams's two plays written under the title of *Garden District,* 'Something Unspoken' and 'Suddenly Last Summer', were forced to go underground and seen only on the stages of private theatre clubs in this country, when calls for the pieces to be banned were heard.

The staging in Leeds, during week commencing April 4, 1960, coincided with the release in London of the film *Suddenly Last Summer* starring Elizabeth Taylor and Katharine Hepburn. Jean Tordoff gave an impressive performance as Catherine Holly, the girl who goes insane after witnessing her gay poet cousin being raped and murdered by beach boys. Vivienne Jacobs was also excellent as the boy's mother who attempts to wipe out the trauma from Catherine's brain by lobotomy. The play drew in large audiences and received critical acclaim and Cyril brought a huge amount of sensitivity to the piece.

For their next production in November, 1960, Anita Silverton was given her first directorial job in Schiller's *Mary Stuart*. She made a tremendous success out of it. The show was the most lavishly costumed production seen at the Civic for years. Jean Tordoff made a superbly tragic Mary Queen of Scots while Myrtle Young stole the show as a formidable and austere Elizabeth 1.

The show required extra rehearsal time and when the Arts Guild rehearsals rooms were not available the Society was literally driven underground. The prompter for the show, Barbara Sher, suggested that the group use premises owned by her brother, and gained permission for them to occupy the cellar beneath the bar of the Pop In Coffee Bar in Kirkgate. The Club had been closed for over six months and the space made an ideal rehearsal venue.

I Always Come Here For My Hot Water Bottles
Hotel Paradiso

The Players had never done a French farce before and Cyril thought the Georges Feydeau and Maurice Desvalliers classic *Hotel Paradiso* would fit the bill. The production opened week commencing Monday February 6, 1961.

I was cast in the leading part of architect Boniface, a role that Sir Alec Guinness played on the London stage. Thelma Rose, Myrtle Young and newcomer Jim Wooton also played principal roles. During rehearsals I was having problems devising a way of getting rid of the soot I would acquire on my face after sticking my head up a chimney. I had to appear in a scene immediately afterwards clean-faced and spotless. I could not figure out how to overcome this difficulty so I wrote to Sir Alec at the Haymarket Theatre in London, where he was appearing as Lawrence of Arabia in the play, *Ross*. Sir Alec wrote back, in his own hand, with details on how to resolve the problem and the story was used to excellent effect in the local press, giving me a hankering for thinking up future publicity stunts and stories. Cyril set up a special workshop to create the quickfire comedy timing needed for the piece. Some of the scenes between Thelma Rose and I were caught on film by Bernard D. Skibben after Cyril had suggested the rest of the company observe our style of comedy. Thelma and I were highly amused and felt, for a short time, terribly grand and important. Cyril's production built up to a highly amusing hotel scene where all the characters in the play appear to have made clandestine assignations. All was revealed, however, with the whole company running about the stage and throwing up their hands declaiming: 'What a night! What a night!'

Writing in the *Yorkshire Post*, Desmond Pratt noted that not only was the production excellently staged but the acting was impeccably executed, being all the more remarkable coming from a society not versed in the art of comic acting.

Carole Morris (nee Manning) remembered joining the Pross when she was about 17. 'I had made two friends at the Moor Allerton Golf Club, Judith Caplan (nee Brostoff) who had already worked backstage and Dale Cowan (nee Pinkerton). I had already been involved with drama at school, notably appearing as Puck in *A Midsummer's Night Dream* and a small speaking part of a schoolgirl in *Quality Street*. Both of my pals were excited about joining the 'best drama group in Leeds'. We were overawed by the standards the group achieved; there were some superb actors and we all knew that Cyril Livingstone was the best director around because he kept telling us so! We felt as though we had joined some up-market performing arts academy and we learned so much.

'I'll never forget the excitement I felt when I received a type-written letter offering me the part of Marguerite, one of the four daughters of Monsieur Martin, a barrister who always stammered when the rains fell and was played hilariously by James Rogers.

'Appearing in the play was the most wonderful experience. The part suited me down to the ground; a naughty little girl prancing around the stage talking about using her curling tongs. My mother provided the tongs as she was a hairdresser. She came to see me three times, she was so proud.'

Writing in the programme, Cyril said that following the policy of the group new members should serve their apprenticeship backstage and the Pross was delighted that some of them had been able to take part in this production. 'Judith Brostoff, Marjorie Petty and Dale Pinkerton had proved their enthusiasm and efficiency on the technical team and were now rewarded with speaking parts,' he said.

Cyril also welcomed two actors from the wider community, James Rogers, who acted for over ten years with the Slazenger Players, and Jim Wootton, who appeared with the Port Sunlight Players and the Green Room in Liverpool.

Cyril followed this production in April 1961 with a tense drama adapted by American playwright Lillian Hellman called *Montserrat*, from a French play by Emmanuel Robles. It dealt with the Spanish occupation in 1812 of Venezuela and General Bolivar's uprising. One man, Captain Montserrat, of the Spanish forces, turns traitor and assists Bolivar. He is captured by the Spanish army and refuses to give information, so five innocent people are dragged from the streets and held hostage. They are given just one hour to persuade Montserrat to provide the army with information as to Bolivar's whereabouts or each one would be executed. Tension builds as we wait to see the results. The way in which the hostages deal with each other and come to grips with the situation is moving and realistic.

Above: Gerry Riche, John Fisher and Peter Buntman in *A Man For All Seasons*, 1963

Leslie Wainwright again designed a superb box set painted overall in white, with an impressive flight of stairs, stage left. Nevil Silverton was also in inspirational mood when he lit the stage in dramatic blue filters that gave the impression of heat.

The actor who was to play Salas Ina, one of the hostages, dropped out two weeks before the play opened and Cyril took over the role, which he played admirably. Julia Jonathan, from *Under Milk Wood*, played Matilde, and in the cast as Luhan was Canadian actor Steve Callahan, who was a University student. I was cast as Colonel Izquierdo. It was quite a sizeable part and very dramatic. I had already played the lead in *Hotel Paradiso* and here I was again, never off stage for a second. It was a terrific role though and I think I rather relished it.

The *Yorkshire Evening Post* thought the company handled the play with courage and audacity. It praised Allan Pliener who played the leading role and liked Frederick May's performance as Juan Salcedo Alvarez, a renowned actor in the grand tradition and then added: 'It was an explosive drama in which any actor worth his salt will revel. For sheer acting ability and sweeping everyone else on stage aside, there is John Fisher as Colonel Izquierdo, a satanic officer who leans over men's shoulders as if he were Lucifer tempting Christ.' I dined out on that review for many months to come and needless to say Izquierdo proved to be one of my favourite roles.

Cyril was in fine form again when the Players returned to the Civic Theatre in October 1961 with Arnold Wesker's *Roots*. The play was already famous from Joan Plowright's brilliant performance at the Royal Court Theatre in London and the production attracted theatregoers from around the region. In preparation, Cyril wanted the Norfolk accent to sound authentic so he arranged for the cast to be coached by someone from that region. Jean Tordoff launched into the key part with gusto presenting a very fine Beattie Bryant. The *Yorkshire Post* thought *Roots* full of fine character actors, including Nora Wigglesworth and James Rogers who played Beattie's parents.

Anita Silverton was then appointed to direct a magnificent production of Dostoevsky's *Crime and Punishment* during the week commencing February 12, 1962. The play had been dramatised by Rodney Ackland and the Pross gathered a company of some 40 actors. For the part of Rodion Romanovitch Raskolnickoff, the Players cast a young, talented actor/student at Leeds University called Ronald Pickup. Pickup's performance as the young Russian decorator, who murders for money and power, was to bring him much praise and many admirers, including Frank Hauser from Oxford Playhouse. Ron's mind was made up, however, for he was preparing to audition for a scholarship to RADA.

During the week of the show, he tried out one or two of his test-speeches backstage and won the approval of his peers. There was no doubt that this young actor was destined for bigger things and we all knew that there was another Peter O'Toole in the making. Ron even attempted to persuade me to go down to London and try for a RADA audition. 'Perhaps you are too old for a scholarship, but I think you'd pass the entrance exam,' he said.

I got as far as sending for the prospectus and the necessary papers and even had a photograph taken at Scrimshaw's for their files but, after much thought, I declined.

Ron was eventually to be awarded a scholarship that led to a trailblazing, glittering career, acting at the National Theatre, appearing in the West End, on radio and TV and the chance to act opposite Sir Laurence Olivier and Constance Cummings in a definitive production of *Long Day's Journey Into Night*, firstly at the National and then in a successful West End transfer.

Crime and Punishment was hailed as a terrific success and because of Pickup's performance brought in a new audience eager to see a future star in the making. The *YEP* predicted that the production would be remembered as a classic production by all who saw it. 'Rich in the sordid, bawdy, rude atmosphere of Russia under the Czar, Silverton's production told the story as movingly as anything we shall see outside the professional sphere'.

The critic continued to say that the great strength of the production rested on excellent acting and observed that Pickup played the part with wild, staring eyes and taut face; his lapses into depression made his portrayal unusually impressive and outstanding. Jane Platt, as his mother Katerina, a woman clinging to the skirts of a former glory, also came in for praise as did Cyril Livingstone's Chief of Police. 'Like a sleek cat approaching a saucer of cream he relished his role and left us licking our lips'. Regional theatre reviewing

Above: Peter Gallagher, Cyril Livingstone, Myrtle Young, John Fisher and Jean Tordoff in *The Fire Raisers*, April 1963 at Leeds Civic Theatre

doesn't get more descriptive than that. I played the role of Looshin, suitor to Dounia Romanovna (played by Thelma Rose). At rehearsals the director said I looked too young for the part (that made a change) and persuaded me to wear body padding to alter my stance. Apart from an elaborate make-up I was encouraged to sport a thick shirt and a beautiful chunky Jaeger sweater which I had just purchased at men's outfitters Brill's for the sum of three guineas.

We ordered a costume two sizes larger and the make-over certainly made me look fatter but by the end of the week's run I discovered I had lost three pounds in weight.

It was in the summer of 1962 that I was invited to perform in my second Leeds University Rag Revue and nearly got myself banned from appearing at Leeds City Varieties where it was staged.

In the show I was given a sketch to do involving an

impersonation of Prime Minister Harold Macmillan. It was a satirical piece where, following a huge explosion on stage, I gave a speech outside a bunker after a nuclear holocaust. Everything was fine in rehearsals until the producers sent the show's manuscript to the Lord Chamberlain for sanction. He duly approved everything except my sketch which he banned for being too subversive. (Well, it was a University show, after all). 'Mack's the Word' was due to be the show's high-spot and the decision left the whole revue in turmoil because the ruling arrived just a few days before opening night. An emergency meeting was held and we agreed to use an amended script, written by the Lord Chamberlain's office, which had to be specially flown to us from London to Leeds.

If this example of censorship wasn't bad enough, the Lord Chamberlain also demanded another requirement; I had to wear a rubber mask during the sketch because impersonating a politician was forbidden.

The fuss surrounding the sketch seems comical by current standards. At that time we all felt the banning decision was biased because Peter Cook was able to do an impersonation of the Prime Minister in the revue *Beyond the Fringe* in the West End. We all thought we were caught up in the old North-South divide syndrome. However, I absolutely refused to wear the rubber mask, which looked ludicrous and smelled disgusting; although I did abide by the censored script. The story went national with headlines like: 'Leeds actor's sketch axed by Lord Chamberlain' and 'Leeds University Macmillan Send-Up Censored', as well as 'Proscenium actor told to Wear Mask', which I suppose was all good PR. The revue was directed by Martin Glynne and Pross players Val Gallagher, Wilf Carr and Sue Goldie were also in the company.

The Pross had not presented a play with a Jewish theme since *The Diary of Anne Frank* and when a script from Israel arrived about another Jewish heroine, Hannah Senesh, the group jumped at the chance to present it as their October 1962 production.

Unfortunately, Aaron Meged's play *Hannah Senesh* was not in the same league as Goodrich and Hackett's classic. It had been premiered in South Africa and then staged in Israel where it had received a moderate success. However, as the play was to be a European premiere Jewish charity groups in Leeds were all keen to support it and the production went ahead. Director Cyril was in Israel during the preparatory stages and decided to call upon Meged and get his thoughts on how the production should be presented.

The play was about a young Hungarian Jewess, who, in 1939, left her wealthy Budapest home to work in the settlement. When news filtered through of the extermination of Jews by the Nazis, she joined the British underground movement, training initially as a young parachutist. She re-entered Hungary to form an escape route for Jews from Hungary and the Balkans. When Hannah was eventually captured, beaten and tortured by the Hungarian pro-Nazi forces, she refused to reveal the code used by her fellow partisans and was executed.

Playing the leading role was a young local actress called Catharine Hyams, niece to Oxford Playhouse's dynamic artistic director Frank Hauser. Catharine played the part with as much sincerity as she could muster from Meged's sluggish writing and managed to convey something of Hannah's energy. The more experienced actress Myrtle Young brought a warmth and sincerity to the role of Hannah's mother.

Desmond Pratt thought that Meged's writing showed no sense of dramatic unity, lacking tension and menace, and that some of the actors were unable to connect with the piece. Even so, as a result of the interest shown by local Jewish charities *Hannah Senesh* proved to be a financial success.

What Is The Man?
A Butcher's Son!
A Man For All Seasons

Flushed with her *Crime and Punishment* triumph, Anita Silverton was now making quite a name for herself as a director and Robert Bolt's costume drama, *A Man for all Seasons,* suited her penchant for historical plays down to the ground. During the week commencing February 4, 1963 she managed to produce another great big hit and added Bolt's drama to her growing list of successes.

The title of the play was taken from a passage that was composed for Tudor schoolboys to put into Latin - 'More is a man of an angel's wit and singular learning: I know not his fellow… a man for all seasons.'

Leslie Wainwright designed a functional set with clever lighting by Paul Clarkson. Kirkstall Abbey House Museum agreed to loan us the period furniture and the beautiful costumes were supplied by Nathan's in London.

The press thought the production ranked with the season's best and commented that the group had assembled one of the strongest amateur casts ever seen on the Leeds stage.

John Brewster, as Thomas More, proved himself to be an actor of considerable merit and gave a tremendous performance. His chief asset was his melodious voice which did justice to the compelling dialogue. The *YEP* thought his More was a towering figure both physically and spiritually. Gerry Riche brought a wry, sly touch to the role of the narrator, The Common Man, while David Leslie, an actor usually associated with musicals, turned in a very showy performance as King Henry Eighth. Veronica Whitham also impressed as More's wife Alice. I played the Spanish Ambassador and wore a fantastic black studded sparkling costume that would not have looked out of place in the BBC's *Strictly Come Dancing*.

Some historians criticised the play's portrayal of More as a Saint, noting that Bolt mentions none of More's negative activities such as his persecution of Lutherans while serving as Chancellor.

A newcomer to the group was Nevil Tolkin who was brought in to join the backstage crew. Nevil had been introduced to the Pross by Ralph Ross, who was in charge of backstage lighting and sound. Nevil had already been involved with the technical team of *Crime and Punishment*.

'Ralph thought that because I was a lighting retailer I would be an asset to the team,' he says. 'One of my tasks during the final act was to climb the ladders in the flies, crawl along the gantry so that I was above the centre of the stage and at the moment Cranmer was executed I had to throw down a red cloak which signified his downfall and eventual rise to heaven. The play ran for five nights and for four of those performances that cloak had a mind of its own landing either in the orchestra pit or the front rows of the stalls. An inquest was held after each performance and Anita continually tore a strip off me for failing to position the cloak correctly.

'The final act of the last performance loomed and shaking like a leaf I climbed the ladders, and once more took up my position to drop the cloak. On cue I released the garment and to my amazement it floated down majestically and made a perfect landing on the correct spot. I was ecstatic. At the party after the show I smugly anticipated the praise I felt sure would be heaped upon me. But not a word was said by anyone and dejectedly I exited left and vowed never to darken the backstage of a theatre again.'

In April 1963, Alec Baron was tempted to return to his role as a director. Since the early '60s, Alec had become involved in the Leeds Theatre Campaign, a crusade to build a Playhouse for Leeds. By now, two Leeds theatres had been demolished and were greatly missed, Leeds Empire and the Theatre Royal, both of which had been pulled down and sold to property developers. This was a full time job for Alec who worked arduously for many years on the LTC, eventually reaping rewards when the Leeds Playhouse opened on the Leeds University campus and he was appointed the theatre's Administrator.

For his directorial comeback, Alec chose to do a short Shalom Aleichem piece called *A Tale of Chelm*. This was performed as a double bill with Max Frisch's *The Fire Raisers*.

Chelm had recently been produced in a successful production of Shalom Aleichem plays in the West End and was a nice folk story that Alec played in the style of the Yiddish Theatre. In a brilliant cast Michael Kent was ideal as Mendele the old bookseller and Thelma Rose was hilarious as the Angel Rochele, experiencing great tribulations adjusting her wings. Val Gallagher, an actor who had been involved with the Pross for some years was given his chance to direct the Frisch and made a wonderful job of it.

Max Frisch's drama made many points, political and moral, about the situation in Europe as it was then. The confrontation between the two fire raisers and the owner of a wealthy suburban house led to a flaming climax, and actors Cyril Livingstone, Peter Gallagher and myself rose to the challenge.

Joan Gordon remembers being in charge of props for *The Fire Raisers*. 'Actually it was one of the few plays I disliked,' she says. 'I am terrified of fire and I also hated the surrealistic element of the play's theme - that quiet genteel goodness is no match for evil. However, the play did send a strong message for people to become more involved in what was going on around them and not to be bystanders.'

Nevertheless, Joan concentrated on her props and recalls that she had loaned her one and only white tablecloth to be used in the play. 'I had the cloth ready in the on-stage sideboard for the maid (Jean Tordoff) to place on the dining-table as part of the action. On the first night all went well but I thought the cloth looked a little grubby, so after the performance I duly took it home to launder ready for the end of the week. We had one in reserve because Myrtle Young had given me her own tablecloth, so I placed that in the sideboard ready for the second night. However, when the time came for the maid to unfold the cloth onto the table I cringed because the material went on unfolding for what seemed forever and a day, culminating in a huge heap on the floor. I'd forgotten Myrtle's dining table was much longer than mine!'

For a long time Alec had been enthusiastic about the work of Bertolt Brecht. His burning desire was to do Brecht's three major plays, *The Life of Galileo, Mother Courage* and *The Caucasian Chalk Circle,* in one season. The committee, however, was dubious and after quite a one-sided battle by Alec, the idea was shelved. He had first mentioned *Mother*

Courage five years previously and had he received the executive support The Pross would have been credited with the British Premiere of Brecht's work. Yet times and committees change and in November 1963 *The Life of Galileo* received its Northern premiere. Alec used the Charles Laughton adaptation on which Brecht himself had assisted.

It was an epic play needing over 40 actors, mostly men. In the title role Peter Cariss excelled, and his performance was to be remembered by theatregoers for many years to come. The play came under the critical eye of John Wood, the Director of Further Education in Leeds, who wrote a scathing letter to the *Yorkshire Post*.

'...You give seven-and-a-half inches to a notice of the annual exhibition of the Royal Academy and only two inches under the sub-heading Civic Theatre, Leeds, to the Proscenium Players' production of Brecht's *Galileo*,' he wrote. 'I have twice seen the play produced professionally but this week's production was to me the more illuminating, the more memorable and the more truly professional. It deserved space equally for a critical appreciation as a theatrical occasion and as an event in local life.'

Mr Wood's letter, which brought him much support, covered a notable three columns and ironically measured an impressive nine-and-a-half inches.

In February 1964, Cyril Livingstone directed William Gibson's *The Miracle Worker*. This was the play about Helen Keller, who was deaf and blind since the age of 19 months as the result of an illness. She was educated and guided by Boston teacher Annie Sullivan, who was once visually impaired. Although the play was a smash hit on Broadway and later made into a successful film starring Anne Bancroft as the teacher, the press in Leeds thought the play wasn't strong enough.

The *YEP* observed: 'To hold the interest of an audience

for almost two and a half hours with a weak play is no mean achievement. Yet this is what the Proscenium Players succeed in doing with their fine performance.' Newcomer Patricia White played Annie Sullivan, while little Betty Tunstall as Helen Keller made an impressive debut.

Alec Baron returned in October 1964 with a hugely entertaining production of Brecht's *The Caucasian Chalk Circle*. Once more, the Brecht called for a large cast and Peter Cariss once again shone, this time in the part of Azdak, the village scribe, later to be elected as Judge. His performance was masterly and he proved, if proof was needed, what a fine actor he was.

Also in the cast was a young actor from Leeds University who showed much promise. This was Neil Cunningham, as Shalva, the Governor's adjutant. After this production Neil decided to turn professional and worked for many years in provincial rep, later coming into the West End and TV. Others in the piece were Veronica Whitham, Val Gallagher and Diane Gaunt. Gwen Hart excelled as Grusche Vachnadze, the heroine of the piece. The decor was by Patrick Oliver, Michael Kent and Alec Baron, while Sid and Hadassah Singer (Alec's sister-in-law and her husband) wrote the music for the songs. Josephine Glynne, a trained ballet dancer, arranged the choreography for the dances.

The play was a prime example of Brecht's epic theatre and was a parable about a peasant girl who steals a baby but becomes a better mother than the child's natural parents. Written in 1944 when Brecht was living in the US, the setting of the play was clearly Georgia although it is described as Grusinia, a Russian variant name.

In January 1965, Cyril Livingstone directed a modern dress version of Ben Jonson's *The Alchemist*. The play was written in 1610 and Cyril felt that it showed very clearly that human nature never changes. If we do not entirely believe in the Philosopher's Stone, which turns base metal into gold, we had its modern equivalents, like gambling.

Some approach a classical play with traditional romantic fervour and reverence, but Cyril thought that it had such a close parallel to contemporary life that modern dress was justifiable. Consequently there were quite a few alterations in the text; taxi being used instead of coach and horses.

Wilf Carr (later to turn professional using the name Jack Carr) played Face and Peter Gallagher was Subtle. Both played their parts with enthusiasm and energy and their dressing room was instantly renamed 'Testosterone Towers'. Thelma Rose, in scanty undergarments, made an attractive Doll Common and brought her unique style of comedy to the role.

Production manager for the show was Martin Glynne. There was an amusing incident on the first night, however. Cyril noticed that at the dress rehearsal the landing and flight of stairs looked rather bare and asked Martin to obtain some small painting from Leeds Art Gallery, who had helped furnish the set, to make it look more interesting.

It was 5.30pm and I was in my dressing room on the first night (I was always first in and last out) when suddenly from the stillness of an empty theatre I heard the most awful commotion.

Cyril had come into the auditorium and noticed that the largest and most ornate painting imaginable had been placed on the bare wall of the set. It absolutely dwarfed the decor and was so heavy the flats were almost shaking. Cyril was beside himself with rage and Martin was ordered to remove the offending masterpiece at once by a director at his most apoplectic.

If Anyone Has A Conscience It's Generally A Guilty One
The Fire Raisers

In May 1965, the Pross chose to present another Max Frisch. Their production of *The Fire Raisers* still lingered in the mind and *Andorra* continued a theme that marked much of the Swiss playwright's work; an examination of an ordinary individual involved in terrible events outside his control.

After World War Two, Frisch had written a small prose sketch, only a few pages long, called *The Andorran Jew*. The content of the piece fascinated him and he eventually developed its theme into a full-length play which became *Andorra*. The play observes the sole Jew in a provincial small town, an unsophisticated and naïve youth who chafes under the condescension and outright bias of his neighbours. Although he is not really a Jew, his father has always told him so. Michael Holt played the youth, Andri and John Brewster returned to the group to play the important part of Can, the teacher. There was a chilling scene towards the end of the play when The Jew Detector is called in and the small

Above: The magnificently titled *Little Malcolm and His Struggle Against the Eunuchs*

community comes under his scrutiny. Reluctantly, I accepted the invitation to play the role. There was no dialogue to learn just a sinister presence to capture, and I wore black and a pair of rimless glasses which kept catching the light. For years afterwards people used to refer to my portrayal and it took me a long time to throw off that haunting image. The play was designed and directed by Michael Kent, and Alec Baron was in charge of lighting.

Shortly after this production the society decided to form a play selection committee with a specialist panel that included George Hauger, John Wood, Anne Brewster and Alec Baron. The four panellists had a collective academic and practical theatrical experience which was hard to equal. Among the plays suggested for consideration were *Mother Courage, Life is a Dream,* Hoadly's *Suspicious Husband,* Strindberg's *Dance of Death* and Mercer's TV play *Where the Difference Begins.*

One suggestion from the committee was that the Pross revert to their 1957 policy of presenting four productions a year. Since the late '50s, the group only staged three plays in a season. The possibility that they would extend that output, which included a recommendation that the production of *Mother Courage* would run for two weeks, meant that the group would take the theatre for five weeks in the year, longer than ever before.

Alec Baron returned as director in November 1965 with an inspired production of Brecht's *Mother Courage*. At last Alec's wish to produce this mighty chronicle of the Thirty Years War was to be fulfilled. Alec searched long and hard to find the right actress to play the part of Anna Fierling, the Mother Courage of the title, and at last, the group managed to persuade Audrey Sykes, a leading actress at Bradford Civic Playhouse, to take this mammoth part.

Courage loses all three of her offspring as she becomes a war profiteer. Alec used a lot of alienation devices in accordance with Brecht's instructions. He claimed he wanted to keep audiences intellectually involved rather than concentrate on the emotions of the piece.

Although Audrey was a quiet, slightly introverted person, almost inarticulate in everyday conversation, she had the knack of coming alive on stage. She turned in an unwavering and emotional characterisation and received a wonderful reception from audience and critics alike. The play wasn't to everyone's liking, however, with one theatregoer heard to say: 'That was a cart load of bloody misery,' as he left the first-night performance.

Alec managed to install a full stage revolve into the Civic Theatre, the first time this had been used. There was much difficulty in getting Mother Courage's covered wagon into the building and it was finally hoisted on to the main stage from a yard one floor below through a back window. Alec also formed a small band of musicians comprising piano, flute, trumpet and percussion, to accompany the many songs composed by Paul Dessau. Arnold Morris was the Musical Director.

In February 1966 the Society presented a world stage premiere. Cyril Livingstone's production of David Mercer's *Where the Difference Begins*, proved to be a real feather in the group's cap. Mercer, who was born in Wakefield, had been voted the most promising playwright of 1965 by the *London Evening Standard*. He was the son of a train driver and the play had already been seen on TV, in a truncated form, although it was originally designed to be staged in the theatre.

Where the Difference Begins proved to be one of the best modern plays written in a long time. It was about two sons returning to the family home after their mother's death. Through their confrontation and the ensuing conflict between father and sons was where we find the difference of the title. This starts when the child becomes adult and, in Mercer's view, finds shape between the traditional old and the educated, intellectual new. The play received wonderful press and radio coverage. Mercer himself attended the first night. Desmond Pratt hoped that the play would attract London managements. He felt it was worthy of a West End production.

Benedict Nightingale writing in the *Guardian* thought the play was quite a coup for the group. 'They face it manfully,' he wrote, and admired Mercer's writing, particularly of the Yorkshire people. He singled out for praise 'one, sad, grisly scene amid moribund Darbys and Joans, excellently played by John Fisher and Vivienne Jacobs. Their scene was genuinely felt and rendered with sympathy and dignity.'

Something light, humorous and frothy was certainly needed after the Mercer play and Michael Kent came up

Above: Charles Gardiner and John Fisher in *A Shouting In The Streets*, 1969

with another winner in his production of Eugene Labiche and Marc-Michel's hilarious *An Italian Straw Hat*.

Presented in May 1966, the play revolves around our hero when he is prevented from attending a friend's wedding after his horse chews up a lady's hat and her escort demands he chase around finding a replacement.

It had a cast of 30 and Peter Gallagher was praised for his performance as the market gardener, Nonancourt. Veronica Whitham turned in a nice performance as the milliner Clara and others who shone were Nora Wigglesworth as Baroness de Champigny and Charles Byrne as landowner Fadinard.

The décor, by Michael Kent and Alan Gliddon, was beautiful, as were the costumes. There was a delightful sense of style and enjoyment throughout the whole production. It was almost like an Italian version of a *Carry On* film.

Cyril Livingstone's production of Tennessee Williams' *The Night of the Iguana* followed in November, 1966, and received high praise. This was to be the play's British northern amateur premiere. An iguana is a large Mexican lizard which the natives tie to a pole until it is ready to be eaten, and William's characters were similarly tethered.

In 1940's Mexico, ex-minister Rev T. Lawrence Shannon has been locked out of his church after characterising the image of God as a senile delinquent during one of his sermons. Shannon is defrocked and has a mental breakdown. Sometime later he obtains employment as a tour guide for a third-rate travel agency. When the play opens he is seen arriving at a hotel in Mexico with a group of tourists, but there is a lot of anger and resentment about his behaviour from the group and a rumour of the rape of a 16-year-old girl.

Desmond Pratt, writing in the *Yorkshire Post*, said that:

> Geoffrey Burnley, a newcomer to the group, gave an impressively angry performance as the unfrocked priest. Marian Walker, acting with the Pross for the first time, played the artist Hannah with a composed pain; travelling with her 101-year-old grandfather poet Jonathan Coffin, accomplishing his last poem at the moment of his death (another of John Fisher's accomplished studies) but all are lost. Myrtle Young, acting against type, played Maxine, the sexually-repressed owner of the hotel. If the first act is over-wordy the bricks that are laid by this master builder of plays fit together in the second act.

Pratt continued to say that Cyril's production was staged brilliantly, but tended too much to comedy in the first act, failing to suggest the tension that existed in the torrid heat of the Mexican scene. However his second act, he thought, was sympathetic and perfect, moving to the great quiet climax of the falling end.

The Final Curtain

Damian Killeen, a young actor who had appeared in one or two previous Pross productions, was given the opportunity to direct his first play for the group and came up with Calderon de la Barca's *Life is a Dream*, staged in February 1967.

Basil, King of Poland, had imprisoned his son Segismund since birth because he had read in the stars that if he became King his reign would be filled with cruelties and disasters. Segismund had only one contact with the outside world, Clotaldo, one of King Basil's trusted courtiers. Some years later, the ageing King decides to give his teenage son the opportunity to demonstrate whether he would be a good ruler and arranges to have him drugged in prison and for him to wake up a prince in the palace.

Apart from doing a fine job as director, Damian also played the part of Segismund. The production gave a young and energetic cast the chance to show what they could do, and generally they came up trumps. The sets were designed by Michael Kent and the lighting was by Pamela Rattee.

Following this production in April 1967 was Ibsen's powerful play *Brand*, with a barnstorming performance by Ian Rattee. A skilful interpretation of David Halliwell's *Little Malcolm and His Struggle Against the Eunuchs* was chosen to open the Pross' 20th season week commencing November 6, 1967 and was crisply directed by Peter Stansfield.

Little Malcolm Scrawdyke was played by Tom Wild, an interesting actor with a strong stage presence. He played the part of a Huddersfield art student who had been thrown out of college and whose fantastic schemes for the overthrow of the headmaster were expressed in energetic soliloquies. His gaunt, unkempt appearance and his dirty, untidy studio setting for the play likened him to a modern day Fagin.

In the cast was John Tolan, a gifted young actor who played one of the students, Irwin Ingham. John cleverly achieved an unconscious humour which was most appealing. Together with Michael Meer as 'Wick', he is persuaded by Malcolm to leave college and become a faithful supporter of the newly-formed political party called 'Dynamic Erection'. Frances Brozel played Ann Gedge, the only female in the play.

The *Yorkshire Post* warned theatregoers that 'this is not a play for those finding pleasure in the euphemisms of the drawing room' but went on to say that 'it is some time since Pross audiences enjoyed themselves as hugely as they did last night'. Jack Dodd, writing in the *YEP*, said the play was a double-decker of comedy and horror and praised Stansfield's firm hand in bringing out talented performances. I played student Dennis Nipple and came in for some great write-ups, 'a gem of a performance' 'hilarious comedy playing' and so on. Meeting up with Alec Baron after the first night he said my interpretation was not quite what Halliwell had in mind when he wrote the part - 'but I bet now he wished it was,' he added.

It was at this time that Harry Hurst was made president of the group, Julian Goldberg chairman and Val Gallagher, a loyal and reliable member was made the group's vice-chairman. I was still on the committee and in charge of patrons and advertisers of which we had over 50.

For many years the group benefited from the advice, assured guidance and business acumen of Julian Goldberg. He brought a solid professional expertise to the Pross in his role as chairman, president, technical advisor and loyal friend. Julian and his wife Mavis left the group to live in Israel in the 1970s and their absence was deeply felt.

An entertaining production of Brendan Behan's *The Hostage,* directed with verve by Michael Kent, was staged week commencing February 12, 1968. Most of the incidents in the play were taken from life though, needless to say, Behan fiddled around with them a lot. The incident of the young British Tommy occurred actually in Belfast but in real life he wasn't shot. This was very much a team play with everyone playing their roles with gusto and style.

That production was soon followed by Noel Coward's masterpiece *Hay Fever* (week commencing April 29, 1968). Directed by Cyril Livingstone, it starred Myrtle Young as Judith Bliss. The action of the play takes place in the hall of the Bliss residence in Cookham in June 1925.

The household of five extroverts in *Hay Fever* were crazy by any standards. Judith was a retired actress basking in her former glories. Add to this her unsuccessful novelist husband David and their two precocious teenage children Simon and Sorel, plus a quirky housekeeper Clara, and you have a wonderful line up of eccentrics. Each member of the family invites a guest down for the weekend and the chaotic results that follow set the play alight.

Myrtle was at home playing high comedy as she was playing the tragic roles, and turned in a classy performance.

Above: John Fisher as Harold Gorringe in Peter Shaffer's *Black Comedy*, 1970

Diane Gaunt as Myra Arundel offered a lovely cameo as an alluring vamp and looked fabulous on stage. I played Richard Greatham, an out-of-his-depth British diplomat and Mavis Goldberg played Jackie Coryton, a 1920s flapper. We both played for laughs and got them!

Frances Glynne (Brozel) remembers the production with great fondness. 'The wonderful Myrtle Young played my mother and I knew from the start that when Cyril took a look at my upper half he was going to, you should pardon the expression, "bind my breasts" because in the Roaring Twenties ladies did not have bosoms. I was also asked to wear a wig. So, at dress rehearsal, my breasts were bound by Myrtle and then this awful, hideous wig arrived on Cyril's arm looking like a bunch of dyed seaweed. Ever the drama queen I announced there was "no way I would wear that thing". Cyril glared at me, then taking my arm he drew me aside and said very

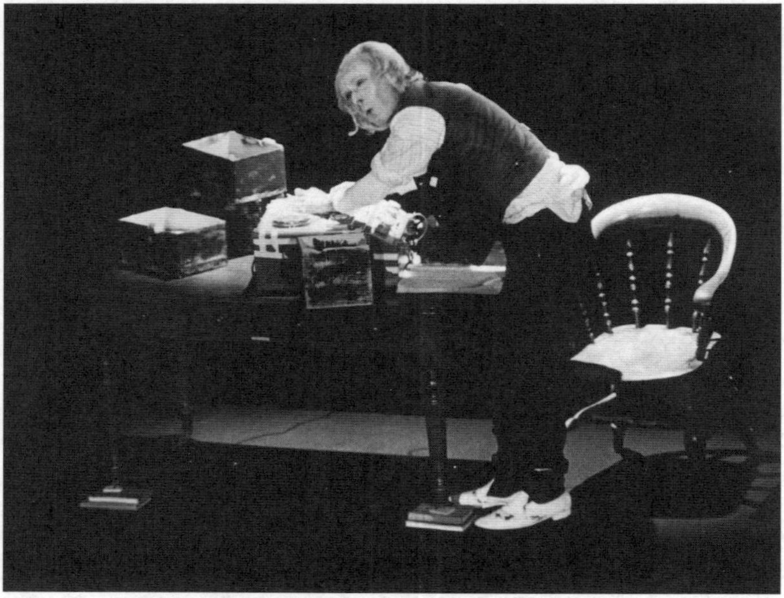

Above: John Fisher brings the curtain down on the Pross with *Krapp's Last Tape*

calmly and quietly: "If you don't wear it my dear, you don't go on. I will replace you instantly and don't think for one moment that I won't." Now only a fool doesn't take notice of a threat like that, so I did as I was told and I think it taught me an awful lot about stage discipline and being professional.'

During the first-night performance, Tom Wild, from *Little Malcolm* fame, remembered sitting in the audience. Act Three opens with the family sitting down to breakfast and kippers and smoked haddock are on the menu. There was a wonderful woman called Sybil Jenkinson who helped occasionally on our technical team and whose job it was to prepare the food. However, on this occasion, Sybil decided to cook the fish the night before but forgot to refrigerate them, so she gave them a quick boil-up.

Tom recalled sniffing the air as soon as the curtain went up. There was a very ancient plump lady sitting on his right

-hand side and he gave her a withering look. However, she just stared back and with a gasp moved slightly over to her companion. Soon the smell became stronger and stronger and everyone in the audience started to sniff and look suspiciously at the person next to them. The audience had become a sea of Bisto kids.

As luck would have it we had the whole of the governing Leeds City Council as our guests, all dressed up to the hilt in evening wear, who had to endure this abominable stench. One well known lady councillor was seen tapping the Lord Mayor on the shoulder and enquiring if he wanted some lavender sprinkling on his 'kerchief. It was all very embarrassing and so un-Noel Coward.

As were the sandwiches we were called upon to eat later on in the tea-party scene. Once more Sybil had prepared the food, a huge plate of sandwiches that was offered to the guests. However, at the dress rehearsal, Cyril had noticed that some of the slices of bread were dropping off the plate and gave Sybil a note to 'do something about keeping them intact'.

So Sybil excelled again with an ingenious solution of sticking them all together with super-glue. She forgot to take into account the sandwiches had to be taken off the plate and eaten, so that when the actors proceeded to remove them they were unable to do so. Those who did accomplish this feat and took a bite came to a very sticky end indeed.

The group was on much safer ground with D. H Lawrence's *The Daughter-in-Law,* which was staged week commencing October 28, 1968 and won much acclaim. Ian Rattee was the director and the small cast of five players did the play great service.

Bertrand Russell described D.H. Lawrence as a man who never allowed himself to bump into reality. However, whatever else he might have been Lawrence was a master craftsman. Ian Rattee said: 'In his coalfield plays Lawrence showed himself the first and now rarely rivalled recorder of working-class life. In the play, the early influences in Lawrence's life may be seen, realistically, warmly, but unsentimentally explored. The theme was simple but the depth and understanding of the people concerned provided a notable theatrical experience.'

Vivienne Jacobs, as Mrs. Gascoigne, played the mother with great sincerity and Maurice Glynne played her son Joe with conviction. Also in the cast were Veronica Whitham, Jean Tordoff and Dennis Stevenson.

A new play by Elizabeth Dawson about racial persecution was enhanced by two terrific performances when guest actors Charles Gardiner and John Linstrum were invited to feature in the amateur premiere of *A Shouting in the Streets* (staged week commencing February 3, 1969).

Set in Lincoln in the 13th century, the drama had a modern relevance. Dawson had chosen a single instance in Lincoln's history of persecution, prejudice and bigotry, none of which had yet been erased from the human scene and her message was that she held no hope that it may be in the future. In 1255, Lincoln had a population of some 5,000 including a very small Jewish community. The play's premise was about a small boy who disappears and is later found dead. The Jews are immediately accused of a ritual sacrifice. Eighteen of the 89 Jews taken to London were presumed guilty because of their refusal to plead and were hanged. The remainder were imprisoned.

Writing in the *Yorkshire Post,* theatre critic Desmond Pratt noticed the modern parallel was easy to see, even though Miss Dawson's play was written long before the recent Iraqi outrages. The dead boy of the play was declared a martyr, subsequently canonised as Little St Hugh and his tomb lay in Lincoln Cathedral. Pratt said Miss Dawson's canvas was too small for a subject as considerable as this. 'Her family scenes, Christian and Jewish, lacked both character and dramatic impact in the dialogue.'

However, he thought the interrogation and torture scenes in the second half had great strength:

> The success lies in the hands of three actors, the weak and frightened Jew of John Fisher; the ageing and dignified Jewish leader from Charles Gardiner, and the ruthless self-centred interrogator of John Linstrum. Behind these three the company play out their grief and anger. However, we should have heard the shouting in the streets but the noise is not contained in Miss Dawson's somewhat cursory look at an incident which could have made a very moving tragedy.

The remains of the tomb of Little St Hugh stands in the passage behind the south wall of the Choir in Lincoln Cathedral. By these remains there is the following plaque headed The Shrine of Little St Hugh...

> *Trumped up stories of ritual murders of Christian boys by Jewish communities were common throughout Europe during the Middle Ages and even much later. These fictions cost many innocent Jews their lives. Lincoln had its own legend, and the alleged victim was buried in the Cathedral. A shrine was erected and the boy was referred to as Little St Hugh. Such stories do not redound to the credit of Christendom and so we pray ...*
> *REMEMBER NOT LORD OUR OFFENCES, NOR THE OFFENCES OF OUR FOREFATHERS.*

The play also gave Barbara Kellerman the chance to appear in a leading role as Judith, my sister. Barbara was later to turn professional, acting with the Royal Shakespeare Company. Among her many credits was appearing in BBC TV's groundbreaking *The Glittering Prizes*. She starred in the feature film *The Sea Wolves* (1980) as Mrs Cromwell opposite Gregory Peck, David Niven, Roger Moore and Trevor Howard. Barbara also scored a huge hit as the White Witch in BBC TV's *The Lion, The Witch and The Wardrobe* (1988). Barbara's parents had fled Nazi Germany and settled in Leeds. Her father was an academic physicist and her mother a senior teacher of modern foreign languages. Barbara and I connected very well and I was tremendously fond of her; she was very beautiful, one of her eyes was blue and the other brown, and she had an exquisite stage presence.

Charles Gardiner, who was headmaster at Intake School, was to recall the play some time later in a lecture on his teaching career presented at Leeds University. He praised the high standards of the Pross and remembered the torture scene in which I died in his arms in the second half. 'There was something in John Fisher's suffering after his torture that I found extremely moving and every night of the performance I was able to cry real tears as he recited the first lines of the Hear O Israel prayer,' he said.

I also remember this scene. It is very hard pretending to 'die beautifully' when a cascade of water splashes down your face every night. I can confirm that when Charles Gardiner cried he really cried salty tears, because I came off stage every night absolutely drenched. He was a delight to play opposite though; charming, sensitive, professional and a real gentle man.

The Restoration of Arnold Middleton was the next production, staged week commencing May 12, 1969. It featured Barbara Kellerman and Martin Glynne, and was directed by Anita Silverton, but it turned out to be a mild success. Written by Wakefield-born David Storey, the play depicted the struggles of teachers who confront crises of breakdown and displacement in their personal lives. The play was first produced at the Royal Court in London in July 1967 and starred Eileen Atkins. Storey was to be voted the *Evening Standard* Award for most promising playwright.

This was followed by a successful staging of *A Kind of Loving*, (week commencing October 27, 1969), adapted for the stage by Stan Barstow and Alfred Bradley and directed by Alec Baron, who had struck up a friendship with both men.

Frances Glynne, who, as Frances Brozel, was cast as the female lead Ingrid Rothwell, recalls it was the production she most liked but not without a certain incident. 'The thing I remembered was a blazing row I had with Alec Baron, who at the dress rehearsal insisted that I strip naked at the end of Act One. He wanted the slip to come off first and then quickly followed by the bra. (Why were all the directors I worked with so obsessed with my bosoms I wondered?) Well, I hadn't been told of this during rehearsals and so I refused. A row occurred and my fiancé Maurice, who was helping with the lighting, took me to one side and said four words to me. "Franny, just say yes." I agreed but only from the first night onwards. So, opening night came round and we had a full house with Stan Barstow and Alfred Bradley sitting on the front row – talk about pressure! I knew Alfred very well, I had been fortunate to do some radio work for him. Anyway, towards the end of the first act the slip came off and then I took a deep breath and reached for the bra fastener. I was just about to let the bra loose when lo and behold the lights went out. Who directed this master stroke I will never know but as my fiancé was in control of the lighting who's to say? That was how it remained for the rest of the run and Alec never mentioned it again.'

Playing opposite her was newcomer Piers Johnson, who

Above: Book ends - John Fisher and Barbara Kellerman in *A Shouting In The Streets*

played Vic Brown. Piers worked in insurance and spent half the rehearsal period trying to sell insurance policies to reluctant members of the cast. Sadly his performance had as much appeal as his insurance. Myrtle Young turned in a nice performance as Mrs Rothwell and I played Mr Van Huyten, whose record shop Vic worked in on a Saturday. It was a nice character part but for some unexplained reason I ended up looking like Mr. Pastry. The set was designed by Pat Olsen and lighting by Trevor Faulkner.

On week commencing February 2, 1970, the Pross presented a double bill that showed off the acting talents of the group, and proved to be a double decker success of farce and tragedy. Edward Albee's *Zoo Story* and Peter Shaffer's *Black*

Comedy brought in full audiences and critical acclaim. The Albee was directed by Cyril and the Shaffer by Michael Kent.

Albee's forthright dialogue with its subtle mixture of pithy comments intertwined with inevitable tragedy was told on a park bench near a zoo in New York's Central Park. It was a horrifying tale of a young man who is desperately lonely, finding no real contact between himself, people or animals. He attaches himself to a mild business man who is reading a book and enjoying what he had anticipated would be a quiet Sunday afternoon in the park. After interrogating the man about his conventional life the young man then gasps out the dreadful bewilderment that infests his own mind.

Bill Tordoff as Jerry, the unfortunate youth, won all the acting plaudits. The *Yorkshire Post* called his a brilliant talent and said Bill gave one of the best individual amateur performances seen in Leeds for years. 'Producer Cyril Livingstone has ensured that every nuance of dialogue is caught. This was a marvellous interplay with heartrending dialogue'.

Black Comedy was a sheer delight and acted out expertly by an enthusiastic cast. It was a superbly funny farce made funnier by contrasting characters. A blown fuse provides the situation when darkness is represented on stage by brilliant light and light being represented by darkness hence the title. The action took place in an apartment in South Kensington and in the cast were Peter Talbot as Brindsley Miller and Sue Carr as Carol Melkett, hilariously all drinkie-poos-and-mummy-and-daddy-darling. I had a whale of a time playing Brindsley's neighbour, Harold Gorringe.

Frances Glynne, who played Clea, recalls the complexity of the rehearsals as well as the performances. 'Michael Kent was a marvellous director and had me timing the removal of my sun glasses on top of other sun glasses to an exact second. I learned more from the Pross under his direction, and that includes Cyril Livingstone of course, than at any time in my career.'

The last Pross production I appeared in was a fine staging of *The Real Inspector Hound,* and Samuel Beckett's *Krapp's Last Tape,* (me again, alone on stage with a tape-recorder and a bunch of bananas), presented in November 1970 as a double bill. The late Nick Clarke, who later became famous as a presenter on Radio 4's *Today* programme, started his career as a cub-reporter for the *Yorkshire Evening Post*. One of his tasks was to write a Leeds Amateur Stage column and follow the groups who performed at the Leeds Civic Theatre.

He wrote about the double bill most enthusiastically: 'Maintaining the very high standard which is now expected of them, the Proscenium Players gave a smooth and polished performance. John Fisher as Magnus Maldoon made a meal out of the melodrama and played with a high seriousness which had the audience in fits of laughter. His Krapp in the Beckett masterpiece was a tour de force.'

By this time it was very clear that things were beginning to wind down. Suddenly there were no more sparks to fly and the lingering and gradual dawning that the final seasons of the Proscenium's 'Old Guard' were drawing to a close was evident. It was becoming increasingly difficult to find actors, directors and administrative staff and, if the truth be told, the writing was certainly on the wall that the future didn't look too good.

Without warning old established members gradually dropped out of the group. The chairman, Julian Goldberg, together with his wife Mavis, who had both made enormous contributions to the Pross, had made plans to live in Israel. Business manager, Dennis Cowen, thought it time to move on and became involved with other projects. Myrtle Young also decided to call it a day, as did founder member Cyril

Livingstone and Anita Silverton. What had once seemed so magical and motivating had suddenly turned sour and so I decided to pack it in too.

A few years later, a few of us started doing 'rehearsed readings' for charity. One charity group who used this genre for fundraising was Leeds WIZO's Rebecca Sieff, a band of stylish and young married women. The events were usually staged at the beautiful Ling Lane home of Kate and Stanley Wootliff.

One play was Wycherley's *The Country Wife,* which was directed by Cyril Livingstone. I played Sparkish and Frances Brozel played the title role of Margery. Frances recalled that we used one actor who was in the original line up of a well-known Yorkshire Television soap. 'He was a sweet man but in his dotage: by this time so gaga he didn't know what he was doing or who he was or who we were and kept losing his place in the script. He kept asking "... and who are you, my dear" and tended to doze off and miss cues, so we had to keep nudging him to wake up.

'My late mother, who had recently had marriage difficulties and separated from her third husband, turned up drunk. I was mortified. She kept telling everyone in the audience, "That's my daughter, she almost got the lead in *A Taste of Honey,* but wasn't ugly enough – and she was directed by David Whitfield." Actually, it was a film test and the director was Tony Richardson.'

Another play we read for charity was Robert Patrick's *Kennedy's Children,* directed by Alec Baron in which Frances played an American hippie-chick. The play originally opened in the back room of a London pub and was discovered - instantly signing for the West End and beyond. It made its Broadway debut in 1975 and won a Tony for actress Shirley Knight. Frances was given a heap of expletives to say, which she delivered brilliantly at rehearsal.

Above: Left to right - Judith Baron on her 80th birthday, Jeff and Thelma Askwith (née Lander) and Cyril Livingstone on his 89th birthday. Cyril and Judith share the same birth date.

When the actual reading was staged, however, Frances's mother turned up and sat on the front row. She was rather short-sighted and tended to glare at people. She wasn't keen on bad language, either; well, not on stage anyway. In those days profanities uttered on TV, stage and film were definitely frowned upon.

Unexpectedly Frances lost her nerve and during her big soliloquy which required a flood of four-letter words she substituted something much, much tamer. 'Mother' was never any the wiser but director Alec was furious. I don't think Frances could have cared less as long as her mum was placated.

The Pross had been handed over to a batch of younger and more enthusiastic actors, including Dale and Gerald Cowen, Ian Rattee, Martin Glynne, Tom Wild and Beverley

Myers, who had new ideas and fresh interpretations and were keen to carry on waving the Proscenium flag.

They decided to keep the group going and liked the idea of retaining the name The Proscenium Players. Their endeavours contributed successfully to the city's amateur stage movement until well into the mid-1990s.

They continued the tradition of presenting plays of quality and interest and presented a diverse programme such as *Jane Eyre,* dramatised by Sally Hunt, and the little known *Les Amants Du Metro* by Jean Paul Tardieu and adapted by Ian Rattee. The play was a great success and picked up the trophy for Best New Play at Harrogate Drama Festival in 1993.

Stepping Out and *Billy Liar* were also highly popular, as were Harold Brighouse's *Zack* and Peter Shaffer's *Amadeus.* A bunch of talented directors was gathered, including Richard and Pauline Noakes, Mike Tordoff, Martin Glynne, Millie Crammer and Jean Adams. There was also a staging of Weill's *Threepenny Opera* directed by Martin Banham.

About this time, the group had an influx of members from Yorkshire Television, including Nick Gray, who was a director of early *Emmerdale,* and who continued his role as director of the group. Nick was responsible for bringing in a well-known TV actor called Toke Townley, who played the part of Sam in *Emmerdale.* Toke played Sir Oliver Surface in the 1979 production of *The School for Scandal.* It was this production that also introduced the stage debut of actress Beverley Callard, who was to go on and create the role of Liz MacDonald in Granada TV's *Coronation Street.*

During this period, historian and presenter Michael Wood, at the start of a successful career, was invited to play Benedict in *Measure for Measure,* directed by Nick Gray before, gradually, the group eventually folded.

Meanwhile, a radical make-over awaited the original

Mechanics Institute in Cookridge Street, as plans developed to turn the building into a prestigious state-of the-art tourist attraction, the City of Leeds Museum. Thanks to a heritage Lottery Grant the theatre and the rest of the building were to become a permanent home for the old Leeds Museum.

However, when plans were announced by Leeds City Council, it was obvious that the Leeds amateur stage movement would be without a home. The societies, supported by their patrons and subscribers who used the Civic Theatre, campaigned vociferously against the closure of the building, helped hugely by the *Yorkshire Evening Post*.

Once all the letters of protest and arguments for securing the theatre for Leeds caught their attention, the local council agreed the amateur stage movement, now sadly depleted, was worthy of preservation. They finally agreed to provide alternative accommodation and built a brand new theatre and conference hall just opposite in Millennium Square. The Carriageworks Theatre housed in the historic Electric Press building cost in the region of £12million and is a 350-seated main auditorium with an additional 80-seat studio theatre. It opened its doors on October 17, 2005.

Leeds Civic Theatre, home to some of the best amateur productions in the country, rung down its final curtain in May 2005 with a performance by The Children's Theatre of *Peter Pan* - a fitting ending to a magnificent era.

Above: Proscenium Players founder Alec Baron, with with personal assistant Rita Price on the set of *Juno and the Paycock*, December 1949